Creative Ways to Teach Pr

To Shazia
Best of luck with
your creative
teaching.

Jon Board

Creative Ways to Teach Primary Science

Alan Cross and Jon Board

Open University Press

Open University Press
McGraw-Hill Education
McGraw-Hill House
Shoppenhangers Road
Maidenhead
Berkshire
England
SL6 2QL

email: enquiries@openup.co.uk
world wide web: www.openup.co.uk

and Two Penn Plaza, New York, NY 10121-2289, USA

First published 2014

A catalogue record of this book is available from the British Library

ISBN-13: 978-0-33-524765-3 (pb)
ISBN-10: 0-33-524765-2 (pb)
eISBN: 978-0-33-524766-0

Library of Congress Cataloging-in-Publication Data
CIP data applied for

Typesetting and e-book compilations by
RefineCatch Limited, Bungay, Suffolk

Fictitious names of companies, products, people, characters and/or data that may be used
herein (in case studies or in examples) are not intended to represent any real individual,
company, product or event.

Praise for this book

"This is a wonderfully written explanation and justification for creative teaching of primary science. The book calls for teachers to hand over more control of the lesson to the children so that they can be creative through exploration and investigation. Throughout the book suggestions are made for children to work as researchers. Each chapter is underpinned by research which makes the book eminently suitable for tutors and their students. There is a treasure trove of teaching ideas that makes the book useful also for both experienced and inexperienced teachers. The frequent web links open up another dimension to the work. This is an absolutely must read book for anybody involved in primary science education!"

David Barker, Senior Lecturer in Primary Science Education
at Edge Hill University, UK

"If you have ever wanted to find great ideas and teaching tips in one place, or searched endlessly for something a little special or different to spice up a lesson, then this one-stop shop of ways to enhance any science lesson is invaluable. The book really demystifies what it means to make your science teaching creative so all you have to do is dive in and see what works with your pupils!"

Lynne Bianchi, Head of the University of Manchester's Science Education
Research & Innovation Hub, UK

"If we are to nurture great scientists, we need to create imaginative, inspiring and inventive learning opportunities. This book is a really useful collection of teaching strategies and tips for developing a creative learning environment; including thoughtful guidance about how to maximise the potential of learning so that it is truly cross curricular."

Claire Seeley, Member of the Primary Committee Association
of Science Education, UK

Contents

Acknowledgements

The authors would like to thank staff and children at the following schools:

- Harwood Meadows Academy, Bolton
- Mauldeth Road Primary School, Manchester
- The Deans Primary School, Salford
- St Stephen's Primary School, Bolton.

1

Creativity in primary science

Introduction

Society needs young people with developing science skills and knowledge, and part of that is a willingness to be open to new ideas, try new things and constantly search for the best in everything. For us, much of this comes under the heading of creativity and creative approaches to primary science education.

We begin with a note of encouragement and reassurance. 'I'm not creative . . .' is a phrase we commonly hear from adults. We would say that everyone can be creative. This may of course be manifested in different ways and in particular aspects of life, such as gardening or home decoration. Creativity can be developed in all aspects of our lives (NACCCE, 1999). This includes the arts, humanities, maths, English and science, and of course it includes teaching. For us, 'creative' means dealing with or initiating something that is new, unique or different in some way to you as an individual. It is not a case of creating things new to humanity but things that, to you, are new or novel. That said, there is much value in definitions to be found in the literature, such as 'imaginative activity fashioned so as to produce outcomes that are both original and of value' (NACCCE, 1999: 29). What we seek to promote is this imaginative activity by teachers and their pupils.

This book will assist you with approaches and very concrete ideas that you can trial and adapt in your school, in your class with your children. Some suggestions we are sure will work well immediately; others will require development and adaption to suit you, your children, your situation and the part of science you are dealing with. We would argue that the classroom should be a teaching laboratory that constantly adapts to the needs of the learners, and in which the teacher is constantly learning about teaching and learning.

You will be interested in resources that can help you develop creativity. One example is the Creative Little Scientists organization, which shares ideas and resources, and organizes events. Find out more here:

www.creative-little-scientists.eu

Examples of creative science

What is it about the examples below that you would say makes them creative?

Darwin

Darwin's centenary saw one school celebrate with a Darwin topic and a 'Darwin day', when classes went hunting outside the school for signs of plants and animals. Fossils were 'discovered' in a number of sand-filled play pits. Films of Darwin's life at Down House, his voyage on HMS *Beagle*, and his life and works were used along with websites and books as secondary sources in the research for a newspaper article, 'The truth about Darwin'. The project included history, science, dance, art and design, and literacy – including role play, when Darwin was interviewed and photographed.

Crime scene investigation

Children arrive in school to find their class mascot has been stolen. Various clues are discovered – a note, fingerprints, a receipt, a handprint, a shoeprint. The children devise a series of investigations. The teacher teaches them to use chromatography and fingerprints. Data are gathered, samples are matched and the culprit apprehended – the head teacher!

Lucky dip

On arrival to class children select a number and a letter from cards buried in two sand trays. These allocate the children to teams and assign roles within the teams. Each team devises questions related to the new science theme, and then selects a question that will be the basis of their science work.

Alien egg

A large egg is found in the classroom. When it is broken open, a toy alien is found inside with a message from its parents: 'Look after our young, please, while we are travelling. Our planet, Noom, is very warm; your planet is not warm enough for our child, so please find material for a thermal suit.' The children are divided into groups and tasked to investigate materials.

Could you adapt these examples so they provide even better opportunities for creativity?

Creative teachers

In order to develop creativity we may need to rethink our role as teacher. What makes a science lesson creative? Is it the expression of imaginative thought from the learners?

For this to occur their teachers need to adopt methods that will encourage and develop that thought and expression. Sadly, in many educational contexts children are fearful of making errors; this fear kills creativity (Robinson, 2006). The examples in the box above illustrate motivating contexts that allow opportunities for pupils to take a degree of control. The essential ingredient, however, is a teacher who is willing to give pupils space and support in order to explore ideas. This will include scaffolding, with the organization of groups and resources, and guidance about fruitful approaches. It requires the teacher to teach but also to step back in order to increasingly enable the children in their growing personal engagement with the exciting world of science.

In primary science we have a very strong tradition of investigation. In the best cases learners develop their own science investigations and learner creativity is encouraged. Ofsted emphasized this when advocating the maintenance of curiosity in its survey report on school science:

> Science achievement in schools visited was highest when individual pupils were involved in fully planning, carrying out and evaluating investigations that they had, in part, suggested themselves.
>
> (Ofsted, 2013)

As a teacher, creativity can be an overarching feature of your working life. Subjects and lessons often provide the opportunity to experience the pleasure of an idea and its consideration. Can we look at this from a different angle? Is it right? Is it wrong? Does it work? Does it need to be adapted or developed further? This applies not only to what the children are learning but also to us as professional teachers reflecting on learning about teaching. As teachers we all trial new methods in the classroom, so in a way we act as scientists. We trial, we evaluate, we test a hypothesis, we adapt, we adopt or reject ideas. Might we involve learners in the evaluation of new teaching ideas? Could we work with them as a team, effectively researching the best learning methods for this class? This idea ties into metacognition (Flavell, 1979), or knowing about knowing. As teachers, our business is metacognition. What are the methods of learning that work best? How do I know that I understand X? How do various different learners achieve the same learning? Creativity in our approaches to teaching and learning assists us in our learning about learning.

Creativity

When are you creative?

Think about times in your life when you show creativity: with food, in a hobby, at work, gardening, in home decoration?

How are you creative?

Trying new/different ideas, methods, combinations, links, relationships, enabling others?

Can you identify aspects of your life where you already do, or where you might, show your creativity?

Research shows that primary teachers are generally creative people (Longshaw, 2009). This is evident when topics and curricular plans are designed linking subjects together in coherent, meaningful contexts or topics. It is also evident in successful lessons – for example, when the lesson is grounded in the personal experience of learners developing something of their own, e.g. art work, an investigation or a play. Science education surely presents as good an opportunity as any subject to develop creativity. The subject is about developing ideas and understanding, and science education is about developing new ideas and understanding in the minds of others.

For many primary teachers we have encountered, the extent of their personal confidence around creative science teaching appears linked to their general level of confidence as a teacher of science. When teachers feel less confident can they react by seeking greater control? It is our contention that, as a creative teacher, one first needs to have control of the lesson/classroom so that you can actively shift aspects of control into the hands of the children. In this book we hope to show that this is a core principle of creative teaching. It is perhaps counter-intuitive to recognize that the control we as teachers seek is the prerequisite to shifting control to the children (Cross, 2000).

Living
Things

English

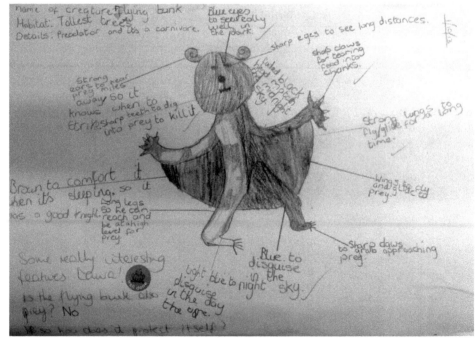

Figure 1.1 Child's imagined creature, suited to its habitat

Science and creativity

An important step at this stage is to think about science and creativity. Think for a moment about scientists you have heard of: Curie, Franklin and others. These people were driven by curiosity, by observing and questioning, by a desire to explain and find out more. Charles Darwin, like others such as Galileo and Copernicus, had to take considerable risks with ideas that were not accepted by many at their time. Their lives can inspire and model creativity in science education and beyond.

Creativity can be threatening. Early people observed the Sun as it appeared to move across the sky, and so assumed that the place they lived was still and that the Sun travelled around it. Copernicus and others challenged this idea and suffered when those around them felt threatened. We now know a great deal about how planets, stars and other objects in space travel in relation to one another, but there is more to learn. Mankind needs creative minds pondering what they see, and suggesting questions and explanations. Can your classroom be a place where creativity is welcomed?

This and the next generation of people living on our relatively small but valuable planet will need to be highly innovative to solve problems and generate ideas that will make lives happy yet sustainable. For all of humanity faced with challenges creativity is going to be very important. People's powers of creativity and innovation will remain key resources in a knowledge-based economy (Robinson, 2000, cited in Grainger and Barnes, 2006).

Sadly, for some, science itself is not seen as a creative endeavour. Some see it as a dry set of facts to be learned. What could be more creative than finding a way to reduce carbon emissions or ensuring that the deaf can experience sound in some way? Creativity itself is not confined to special people or to the subjects we call 'the arts' (Grainger and Barnes, 2006). Creativity is possible whenever human intelligence is engaged (Csikszentmihalyi, 1996). Of course creativity can be used for good and for ill but, like science, it is a force for enlightenment and so we as teachers might see science and creativity as complementary and essential facets of work.

The correct way to consider science is to recognize that it is not a body of facts but a body of theories (Johnson, 2008: 43). The word 'theory' might cause us problems here, so let's substitute the word 'ideas'. A theory is simply our present way of explaining something, but one that will change if new evidence allows us to rewrite or replace the theory. If science is about theories or ideas that can change, then science is about a constant global and/or personal dialogue about each theory or idea. In our lives we have seen the gradual acceptance of the theory that global warming has been dangerously accelerated by human activity. This idea was once on the margins of science, but is now accepted by most scientists. Of course no scientific theory can be proven categorically. Like other ideas it will have to be reviewed if new evidence comes to light. Does this theory continue to predict what we observe? Was the theory unable to account for a recent observation? Do we need a new theory?

What can help me?

Is this discussion assisting you in terms of clarifying the complementary nature of science and creativity? What would you say science is to you?

What is science to you?

closed   <<<<<<<<<<<<<< or >>>>>>>>>>>>>>>   open ended?
belonging to some   <<<<<< or >>>>>>>>>>>>>   belonging to all?
changing   <<<<<<<<<<<<<< or >>>>>>>>>>>>>>>>>>>>>   static?
dull   <<<<<<<<<<<<<<<<< or >>>>>>>>>>>>>>>>   interesting?

What would your learners say?

This book will give you a series of valuable starting points from which to develop creative teaching approaches including pedagogy and with it your confidence to teach primary science very successfully. By success we mean maximum pupil learning, so please don't be fooled by a series of bright ideas presented in any book! It is the pupil learning, which is a product of the interaction between your learners, you and the science they are studying, that will count. Great teaching and teaching ideas are of course like gold – a valuable basic constituent that can then be fashioned to suit a range of purposes and to which value can be added. Creativity can include and underpin a host of highly successful approaches.

It is difficult to identify with any certainty the personal characteristics of creative teachers, although common elements observed in research studies and commented upon by writers in the field (Csikszentmihalyi, 1996; Jones and Wyse, 2013) include the following:

- enthusiasm, passion and commitment
- risk taking
- a clear set of personal values
- willingness to be intuitive and/or introspective
- gregarious and introspective
- a deep curiosity or questioning stance
- awareness of self as a creative being.

National curricula may not always help; they vary, and may or may not promote creativity in pupils (Jones and Wyse, 2013). Curricula can pay lip-service to creativity and then bury teachers in a landslide of facts to be taught, not perhaps encouraging creative approaches. If the curriculum is merely a required set of knowledge, perhaps articulating an aspiration that pupils will understand things and, it is hoped, develop certain skills, it may not prompt teachers to pursue educational objectives about creativity. Some teachers may even think that creativity cannot be taught. We would disagree.

The latest version of the National Curriculum for England (DfE, 2013: 5) does refer to creativity in its general aim, though it suggests a study of the creativity of others rather than a programme to develop creativity in the young:

3.1 The national curriculum provides pupils with an introduction to the essential knowledge that they need to be educated citizens. It introduces pupils to the best that has been thought and said; and helps engender an appreciation of human creativity and achievement.

(DfE, 2013: 5)

Elsewhere in the document creativity is referred to only in the aims of art and design, and in design and technology. It does not appear in reference to other subjects, including English. This we feel is a shortcoming, which we hope readers will want to correct by ensuring creativity in their approach to science. Of course there is an irony here – that we are encouraged to be creative by what is after all a prescribed curriculum (Dann, 2013).

As teachers we can reflect on and develop our ideas around these three things:

1. making science a creative subject
2. learner creativity in all aspects of science
3. teacher creativity in ensuring learner creativity.

Making science a creative subject

All subjects – art and sciences – can be creative. Without creativity these subjects would not be what we see today; western art might still be dominated by unrealistic representations of biblical scenes, science might still see the Earth at the centre of the universe with everything orbiting it!

In writing this chapter we were minded to avoid the term 'creative science' as this feels tautological: science is creative, it has to be, so to use just the term 'science' should be enough. Real science has to be creative.

For primary science teachers it is worth keeping in mind that science is driven by questions. Questions offer a valuable point from which creative approaches can be developed. Children often ask questions that we as teachers might not ask. They often link ideas in ways that we would not. Their naive questions often present excellent starting points for topics, lessons and investigations. This questioning should be encouraged as it is often the product of, or precursor to, creative thought.

However, questions from children often strike fear into the hearts of non-specialist primary teachers. The good news is that these questions can be dealt with by teachers who don't at the time know the answer – for example, by switching the question back to the children as a challenge or recognizing the need to follow the question up with some enquiry. As teachers we need to model that we are comfortable when we don't know an answer, that this state of knowing that we don't know is an important step towards learning. Questions from children should in fact be celebrated as they exemplify truly scientific behaviour. Unknowing is perhaps useful here – that is, knowing what you don't know and asking yourself, That thing that I say I know, do I really know that? Are there aspects I need to revisit or think about?

Questions as opportunities for creative thought

One upper junior class was introduced to a science topic on space and asked, 'What would you like to know about space?' Their responses included:

- How many stars are there?
- How many solar systems are there?
- Where do the stars go in the daytime?
- Is there life on the Moon?
- What is keeping gravity from cracking the universe?
- Why is the universe constantly expanding quicker?
- Who was the first man on the Moon?
- Can lots of asteroids make a planet?
- Is the Sun a big star?
- How old is the Earth?
- What are satellites for?
- Are there aliens?
- Is the Moon grey?
- Does any type of life form live in space?
- Is the Sun the size of 127 planets?
- Is the man in the Moon a myth?
- If a tsunami hit the Sun would it go out?
- What is the Moon made of?
- How big is the Moon?
- How hot is the Sun?

Space

Several of these questions offer the opportunity for children to research. Each one represents a young mind thinking about the world. Seeking answers to these questions would be scientific and would provide scope for creative thought.

This exercise demonstrates the power of the question and the importance of listening.

This elicitation exercise gave a real insight into the understanding of these children.

Hidden among the questions are a number of gems, e.g. *If a tsunami hit the Sun would it go out?* This question might initiate a whole series of enquiries about the Earth, Sun and Moon, about relative sizes, distances and features.

From a list of questions like this, you might assign four or five to different groups in a class.

Source: from a class activity at St Stephen's Primary School, Bolton

Sadly children often ask very few questions. We need to find ways to encourage questions, perhaps celebrating questions as much as we presently do answers.

One approach is to ask learners in pairs or small groups to ask three or four questions about science, pool these as a class and organize them into questions we can answer by:

- research using secondary sources
- talking to people
- conducting surveys
- conducting tests.

The class could then consider any required learning objectives and select questions to tackle.

As teachers we tend to ask questions in lessons, including science lessons. Our questions have a profound influence on learners. Questions can be used to draw and focus attention as well as encourage different thinking. The simple device of the open question is one which enables thought that is expansive. Compare the following:

- What is the second planet from the Sun?
- Tell me what you know and wonder about the inner planets?

Dialogue that is expansive tends to lead to questions – an important step in being scientific.

Learner creativity in science

Take an opportunity to observe, even briefly, the youngest children in your school working in a scientific context. You will observe straightforward, sometimes unrestrained, exploration! This seeming naivety is a characteristic we lose, and it is worth regaining it yourself and reinvigorating it in your children. Create opportunities to observe and ask questions. There is a natural tendency for 10–14 year olds to begin to see the world as not simple but rather complicated, and to feel that, therefore, as learners they have less to contribute (Osbourne and Freyburg, 1985). Sadly this is the opposite of how to learn. As scientists, learners need to engage and ask questions. So in addition to shifting more and more responsibility towards the children – for example, leading investigations – we need to encourage children's question-asking behaviours.

Children developing laws in science

Learners can develop their own laws in science. Here is an example.

Class 4's law of bouncing balls might initially be posted on the classroom wall and read: 'Larger balls bounce highest!' They might then test their 'law' to see if it holds true and perhaps requires review! (See Chapter 2 for more on this.)

Forces

The whole movement of children as researchers provides a great platform for creativity in the curriculum, as learners can see themselves as enquirers rather than receivers of education. In this sense creativity can be taught.

Written with the assessment of pupil creativity in mind, we would suggest that the prompts below (from Redmond, 2005) are highly valuable in articulating the kinds of behaviours we might seek to see in our children. Of course there is a danger in trying to tie creativity down to fit a process.

Imagination with purpose
I can see more than one way of looking at things.
I can create things in my mind.
I ask questions about things that could happen.
I am able to try out new things.
I trust my feelings about things.
I try out lots of different ways to do things and solve problems.
I can compare one thing to another and can make connections between different things.

Originality
I don't always believe things just because everyone else does.
I can find new ways to do things.
I can think of unusual ways of doing things.
I am prepared to try things out even if they might not work.
I like finding out about new things and new ways of doing things.

Value
I can use things I have already learned to help me.
I stop and think about how I am doing in my work.
I can spot problems and ways of dealing with them.
I can see if my work has achieved its purpose.
I can see how other people work to achieve their purposes.

(Redmond, 2005)

These prompts might help teachers and children themselves understand what we mean when we talk about creativity. Of course as teachers we should be wary of trying to pin creativity down to a series of statements – by its very nature creativity should include less tangible elements such as visioning in the head. Visioning for many of us is that mental picture we work with in our heads as we envisage a solution to a question.

Teacher creativity in developing learner creativity

As teachers we soon identify colleagues who we admire for their creativity. These people often display this in particular areas, e.g. planning, classroom display and children's productions. Few teachers have fully developed their personal creativity across the board – indeed, is that possible? Perhaps the first step to being more creative as a teacher is about shifting your state of mind and perhaps your self-image? For some it will start with their developing confidence, so it might be worth beginning in a part of science where you feel most confident.

Your creative times?

Think about times when you have been at your most creative as a teacher.

- In what ways were you being creative?
- At what point of your career did this occur?
- Were you involved in a unique event?
- Were you teaching something new?
- Were you using a resource or approach new to you?
- Were you outside your comfort zone?

Perhaps reflect on your most successful science lessons taught, and those you might have observed. Reflect on these while keeping in mind what is the aim of our science education in primary schools. Is it about developing very positive aspects to enquiry about the world? Are the skills, knowledge and understanding we are told that we have to teach potential vehicles for developing young science enquirers or researchers (see Chapter 2).

You may find it useful to develop creativity in science from other subjects where you have experienced creativity. What is it about creativity in art that makes it creative? Is it the encouragement to try out ideas? To merge ideas? A response to a stimulus? To use a blank sheet of paper or a mass of clay as if nothing has come before? Can we use these approaches in science – to investigations, to questions? Of course we can.

Children in primary schools often love science – they love studying the world around them and participating in practical, hands-on and investigative activity. This positive attitude has been a feature of primary science for years, but has reduced of late (Davies, 2011) perhaps because of the pressure of tests, or an overcrowded or prescribed curriculum?

Can science be seen as playful (Granger and Barnes, 2006; Spendlove and Cross, 2012)? Perhaps more so in the early years. If we are willing to see science as playful, we can try ideas – remember that several major scientific discoveries have been achieved almost by accident! Most of us have heard about Alexander Fleming's discovery of antibiotics after leaving a tray of petri dishes on a window ledge. The key thing was that he saw something that he did not expect and then posed a question.

This is why children need to be happy to accept when their predictions are wrong. They have discovered the unexpected, which is where new science is found – whether that is new science for the world or for the individual.

Forms of creativity

In the section that follows, our intention is to suggest ideas that will make you think about possible approaches. Are these creative in some way? Could these ideas work? It may be worth asking why these have been included here, why would we consider them worth a mention? Do they illustrate a willingness to consider alternatives? How can they be adapted to suit science education?

Teaching idea: Creativity in class

In her article, 'Getting practical', Helen Ward (2011) describes the freezing of leaves and other object in blocks of ice as an opportunity for careful observation of the objects, and how they are affected by the freezing and melting of the water. She also recounts a lesson where a box appears in class containing a letter from an alien asking about life on Earth, questions are posed and a response sought from the class.

Teaching idea: De Bono's hats

A very useful option to help children get into the idea of thinking differently is 'De Bono's hats'. The six coloured hats prompt learners to look at situations, propositions or statements from different thinking angles. The learner puts on an imaginary or physical hat to stimulate thinking in a slightly different way.

1. The **white hat** deals only with facts.
2. The **black hat** considers possible difficulties.
3. The **yellow hat** focuses on positive elements.
4. The **red hat** allows for feelings about the idea to be put forward.
5. The **green hat** offers solutions that may be idealistic or unusual.
6. The **blue hat** is the thinking hat that monitors the thinking of the other hats, and whether/when a solution has been found.

Initially groups of six children might wear a physical hat each and, in turn, the focus of the group moves from hat to hat until the blue hat is reached. Learners support one another, change hats, learning to work and think together.

Find out more about De Bono's hats at:

http://www.debonogroup.com/six_thinking_hats.php
http://www.debonothinkingsystems.com/tools/6hats.htm

Teaching idea: Philosophy for children

Another very powerful thinking environment is provided by P4S, or philosophy for schools/philosophy for children. Philosophy presents children with dilemmas through stories, games and other scenarios. Take the book *The Magic Finger*, by Roald Dahl, in which a girl is horrified by neighbours shooting birds. Her magic finger takes over to swap things around – the hunters find themselves as birds living in nests in tall trees and, below them, are horrified to see duck hunters with guns! The teacher might then lead a discussion around questions such as: Is it right to hunt wild animals? Is it right to seek revenge? How can we approach this without a magic finger?

Teaching idea: Creative Partnerships

Creative Partnerships (2005) was a government-funded initiative. There is no reason why you cannot form creative partnerships with like-minded people. You won't have to look far before you find others who understand the importance of creativity and creativity in science. Options for partnerships include:

- other schools
- other classes
- museums
- theatres
- libraries
- businesses
- universities
- artists
- scientists
- STEM (Science, Technology, Engineering and Maths) groups.

Teaching idea: Flipped classrooms

Some teachers have explored the idea of the flipped classroom, where video and other digital electronic resources are used by teachers to introduce the basic ideas of the lesson. Students study these before the lesson. They then come to the lesson having been exposed to some of the key lesson ideas. The time in class can then be used for the practical application of these ideas. What used to be direct instruction in the classroom is now homework prior to the class – what was once the homework is now the classwork.

Rather than suggest that you adopt the full flipped approach you might consider recorded elements by yourself and/or pupils, which might precede some lessons, perhaps reducing the pressure on class time and freeing up time for more application of the learning.

There is more information here:

http://www.flippedclassroom.com

Flipped teaching

Bergmann provides a clear summary about the nature of flipped teaching:

http://www.thedailyriff.com/articles/the-flipped-class-conversation–689.php

The flipped classroom is not . . .

- a synonym for online videos – when most people hear about the flipped class all they think about are the videos; it is the interaction and the meaningful learning activities that occur during the face-to-face time that are most important
- about replacing teachers with videos
- an online course
- students working without structure
- students spending the entire class staring at a computer screen
- students working in isolation.

The flipped classroom is . . .

- a means to **increase** interaction and personalized **contact time** between students and teachers
- an environment where students take **responsibility for their own learning**
- a **blending** of direct instruction with constructivist learning
- a classroom where students who are **absent** due to illness or extra-curricular activities such as athletics or field trips, don't get left behind
- a class where content is permanently **archived** for review or remediation
- a class where all students are **engaged** in their learning
- a place where all students can get a **personalized** education.

What does the flipped classroom offer us as primary science teachers seeking creativity? At the very least it should encourage us to consider different approaches, and to re-examine the focus of our lessons. Could we develop a series of recorded resources relevant to different ages or stages, which might allow us then to match the instruction to the individual? Would this free up class time for more and, importantly, better-quality dialogue about the particular skill or understanding?

Teaching idea: Reciprocal teaching

Reciprocal teaching is about how the teacher and pupil swap or share the role of teacher. In fact the teacher remains active throughout, helping to structure the lesson. Learners take on the role of 'teacher' as a device to help them formulate ideas through their use of cognitive strategies (the way we approach and solve problems) and support others in the same endeavour.

Reciprocal teaching

Hattie (2009) refers to the effectiveness of this approach in English lessons where the teacher enables learners to learn and use cognitive strategies such as summarizing, questioning, clarifying and predicting. The teacher supports this learning through dialogue and by taking it in turns to be the teacher: learners each take a turn at being the teacher, and themselves utilize and promote the strategies. Reciprocal teaching works best when cognitive strategies are explicitly taught at the start – the strategies are described, modelled.

In science we use similar cognitive strategies, such as observing, questioning, predicting, designing (a survey or research or test), interpreting, concluding. So in this case learners would be reminded about these, they might be modelled, and then learners and teacher would take it turn to lead the class in consideration of these, all supported by the teacher.

For those of us teaching primary science in a creative way, reciprocal teaching is another approach that encourages us to look at the classroom differently and perhaps borrow ideas.

Conclusion

So how will you progress with your teaching to harness the power of creativity? You might adopt strategies that encourage creativity, but you might consider a deeper level of self-review. Consider the following questions.

- How do you view change?
- Do you seek out links?
- Do you notice associations?
- Could you pose questions?

Grainger and Barnes (2006: 5) list six important features a teacher should consider:

1. a learner-centred ethos
2. a questioning stance
3. creating space, time and freedom to make connections
4. employing multi-modal teaching approaches
5. prompting full engagement, ownership and ongoing reflection
6. modelling risk taking, and enabling the children to take risks too.

To be a creative practitioner you will need more than a working knowledge of prescribed curriculum requirements: you will need a secure or strongly developed pedagogical understanding and strong subject knowledge, supported by a passionate belief in the potential of creative teaching to engage, inspire and educate. Such teaching depends in the final analysis upon the human interaction between teacher and student, and our capacity as teachers to allow the learners sufficient space to make errors and gain confidence as creative people.

Chapter summary

- Creativity is personal.
- Everyone can be creative.
- Science is a creative subject.
- Teachers can be creative in different ways.

2

Children as real scientists

What will you learn from this chapter?

- The potential of contexts for real science.
- How children can be real scientists and researchers.
- How children can work with professional scientists.

The teacher's role in science education is pivotal. Teachers usually select the approach to science – for example, the extent to which investigation features, the extent to which it is taught through meaningful contexts.

Opportunities for the learners to take more control can enhance learning. Very good teachers are of course in control of their classrooms, but they use their personal teacher control to shift the emphasis towards the children so that they can take control of the science. The best teachers of science look for ways to enable their learners as scientists. One example of a learner doing science hit the science headlines in 1969.

Tanzanian high school pupil discovers universal freezing effect!

Known as the Mpemba Effect, the fact that hot water freezes faster than cold water sounds counter-intuitive, but it is true and was discovered in 1969 by a high school pupil. He spotted the effect in a cookery class when making ice cream. It is now universally referred to as the Mpemba Effect, named after its discoverer! This effect had been observed previously but was considered by some to be folklore.

Find out more at:

https://medium.com/the-physics-arxiv-blog/d8a2f611e853

http://math.ucr.edu/home/baez/physics/General/hot_water.html#History

http://phys.org/news188801988.html

In this case it was perhaps observation on the part of the pupils that led to the question and then to some tests to begin to consider the effect. The first response can often be, 'Is that really what I saw?', so there is a need to repeat the observation. Following this a science question can be posed. Learners often need support when posing a science question. They may begin with a question such as, 'Which ball bounces best?' One of our skills as a teacher is to help children review and rewrite such questions so that they can be addressed scientifically, e.g. 'Which ball bounces highest?'

Teachers may feel it is appropriate to pose the question or give the pupils a very strong steer. Some readers may have heard of the following example.

Are spiders afraid of conkers?

Primary pupils at Roselyon School, Cornwall, were interested to test the folklore that placing horse chestnut 'conkers' around a house would discourage spiders:

http://www.rsc.org/AboutUs/News/PressReleases/2010/Conkerswin.asp

You can see examples at:

http://www.open.ac.uk/researchprojects/childrens-research-centre/files/crc-pr/file/ecms/web-content/Kara-Burgess.pdf

When learners discover that, actually, no one knows the answer they can be galvanized into action. This might make a teacher feel apprehensive, but this is perhaps unnecessary. When in the classroom the answer is not known learners will be highly motivated to find it. Where teachers model a passion for questions and a determination to answer them, the effect is often infectious.

When you give learners more control you will find that things don't always go as expected. This is much less problematic if you anticipate it and accept that it will happen. In one example Raje and Barleson (2013) asked children to answer the following question: 'If four thermometers were placed in four socks made of different materials and then left in a room for 24 hours what would the temperature on each thermometer read and why?' The children were convinced (wrongly!) that some thermometers would read higher temperatures than others. After the child-led testing, the children initially concluded that the thermometers were faulty! The children were highly engaged and the teacher became aware of their misconceptions, providing the opportunity to challenge them.

This shift towards pupil responsibility is an increase in autonomy; related to independence, autonomy is best defined as self-governance (Baud, 1987). This means that learners are enabled to work sometimes as part of a team and at other times independently. The key thing is that they progressively take control: they can recognize times when it is best to work alone and times when it would be best to work as part of a team.

Pupils contribute directly to the work of professional scientists

Children can assist professional and amateur researchers by gathering data. Perhaps one of the best examples is the annual Big Garden Birdwatch survey organized by the Royal Society for the Protection of Birds (RSPB). Adults and children throughout the UK observe and record birds seen in local areas. This contributes to a large database, which is then published along with a report on the findings. Results are displayed from 30 years of the surveys here:

> https://www.rspb.org.uk/birdwatch/previous-results/
>
> Part of the survey is the Big Schools' Birdwatch survey. For information on this, go to:
>
> http://www.rspb.org.uk/schoolswatch/index.aspx
>
> Other organizations, such as the Natural History Museum in London, have held similar surveys. See:
>
> http://www.nhm.ac.uk/nature-online/british-natural-history/urban-tree-survey/take-part/cherry-survey/
>
> On other occasions, university researchers call upon the assistance of school pupils to gather data. See, for instance:
>
> http://www.bris.ac.uk/biology/news/2009/24.html

Many universities and businesses involved in science run outreach programmes aimed at schools. It can be very worthwhile to get in touch with businesses and university departments to explore options. An example of one such programme organized by the Society of Biology is described in the box on the next page.

National survey of house spiders

The Society of Biology wanted a national survey of house spiders (*Tenenaria sp.*), so it set up a site to help people identify them:

https://s3-eu-west–1.amazonaws.com/sbwebsite/pdf/Formated%20spider%20identification%20document.pdf

and then submit observations:

https://www.surveymonkey.com/s/housespidersurvey

Projects like this offer a clear opportunity for children to contribute to the work of scientists, and to begin to appreciate that science is a world of which we are all part.

For primary learners this is a great opportunity to be involved in and think about the work of researchers. This creative approach is one that might inspire learners in the short term to ask questions and seek answers, but in the longer term to consider other ways that they could find out about and even play a role in research. Most large universities will have some form of community outreach work, which might include the possibility of links to such researchers.

An example of this is the Science and Technology Experts in Primary Schools project, which saw scientists working with children and teachers. To see examples visit the web page of the Primary Science Teaching Trust (PSTT):

> http://www.pstt.org.uk/funding-and-projects/projects/science-and-technology-experts-in-primary-schools-steps.aspx#diaries

Children as researchers

There is a long history of primary school learners enquiring in the context of the curricular subjects and within topics studied. A number of schools and educationalists have explored the possibility of developing children as researchers in a broader sense. In 2004 the Open University established the Children's Research Centre. See:

> http://www.open.ac.uk/researchprojects/childrens-research-centre/

Children researching draws strongly on the investigative skills needed in the various subjects. They can make enquiries and investigations through the arts, through humanities and mathematics investigations, as well as science explorations and investigations. Enquiry skills from history, geography, the arts, maths, science and elsewhere overlap in many ways, but each has unique emphasis, e.g. in history the examination and interpretation of documents and artefacts. They all share a common interest in questions. As creative teachers we might emphasize these similarities and differences, but we can always give the learners more autonomy, particularly as their skills develop.

Learners might investigate questions they identify but might also look at questions prompted, for example, by folklore or received wisdom. For instance, is there any proof for the following?

Red sky at night shepherds delight?
Toast always lands butter side down.
Bananas make other fruit go off.
A halved onion kills smells.
Never water plants in direct sunlight.
Talking to plants helps them grow.
An apple a day keeps the doctor away.
Playing music to plants helps them grow.
Singing brings bad weather.
The pen is mightier than the sword.
Keep pins dry, keep them sharp.
Sunshine makes us happier.

You or learners might look at a selection of these to determine whether science could provide an answer. A question should be formulated; a start might be 'Is it true that . . .?' Then a plan for an investigation can be made and carried out. They might consider whether this can be answered by research of secondary material, a survey or by testing.

Some questions are more philosophical in nature, so while not strictly within the remit of this book they are of course worth pursuing. It might be worth noting that early scientists where known as natural philosophers.

The Philosophy for Children (P4C) website:

http://p4c.com

has free resources including how to run panel discussions (see the 'Sample Resources' section of the website).

The 'children as researchers' movement sees children identifying areas for research and investigation, conducting and then disseminating their findings. The Open University Children's Research Centre organizes events for pupils to talk about their research; it will also publish and assist in the publication of research. For teachers who want to give their classes an audience for their science, blogging – and more especially QuadBlogging (see Chapter 4) – offers access to a real audience who will then interact with you. See:

http://quadblogging.net

Children in control

Learners in science lessons can be very passive recipients of knowledge. As teachers we can strengthen our creative approaches by making the learners scientists. For this to happen we need to shift the control towards the learners. They are not in control of the curriculum in most schools as society and educators tend to take that responsibility, but can we give them some control? Most curricula specify content but not how, where and in what order it will be taught. Can these decisions be shifted towards the learners? We use the word 'towards' as teachers will vary in their willingness to release control. We would encourage any move on your part in this direction. We suspect that you will feel more confident as you trial this approach and become willing to shift more responsibility to the children. One decision we might share with the children is what investigation or research they will carry out. It might help you to let them select the broad area, e.g. friction between surfaces, before you then focus in on a specific question to be addressed.

Metacognition

Learners need to know about their own learning and how they learn best. Along with your class you might create a giant wall poster containing a diagram of the science we know about this topic and the science we are interested to learn about. This might make a useful focus as a learning wall. Sections could be added as lessons progress, and as understanding and knowledge are established.

Misconceptions

As a teacher you will be aware of common misconceptions held by children. One class recently learned about the structure of a flower. They learned to label and describe the function of the parts of a flower. Only in the last lesson did it become clear that the children thought the words 'flower' and 'plant' referred to the same thing! In fact almost everything green was a flower!

By making the children aware of common misconceptions they can recognize that it is not unusual to misconceive something – in fact it might be seen as part of the learning process. Thus misconceptions can be used as metacognitive tools – they can help us to learn.

Writing/thinking frames

Many teachers will utilize writing frames in English and other classes. Numerous writing frames exist to prompt and structure science investigations. We prefer to call them thinking frames as they can prompt and help structure thought around science questions and investigations. These are looked at in much more detail in Chapter 11. There is no doubt however that they can be a great asset when you are attempting to give children more control.

Safety

If learners take control of science they might be given more of a role in considering potential risks to themselves and others. Safety of course remains the responsibility of the teacher. But as most primary science is selected because of the low risk factors, and our suggestion here is that pupils actually discuss and think about safety, our contention would be that this creative approach is probably safer than approaches where children do not think about safety.

Conclusion

For our children, science is their world – it is about the phenomena they encounter and learn about each day. Children are naturally inquisitive so the sooner we can persuade them that they can participate in science the better. This means that their natural creativity can be harnessed as they explore and investigate. Putting them in the driving seat will soon feel very natural to you, and will enable them strongly as researchers and scientists.

Chapter summary

- Shifting control towards the pupils can increase creativity.
- Pupils can work as scientists.
- Groups such as universities will collaborate with schools.

3

A creative approach to working scientifically: putting children in the driving seat

What will you learn from this chapter?

- Why giving children greater responsibility creates effective learning.
- Creative teaching techniques that increase independence.
- How discussion and children's questions lead to a more creative scientific process.

Allowing space for discovery

I remember clearly the delight on Sara's face as she peered into the dark cupboard to collect the seeds planted a few days earlier. 'We've learned something new!' she repeated excitedly as she brought the container to show the class. The seeds, supported by a roll of damp paper in a clear container, had grown roots and some had small shoots. Almost all of the children in this Year 2 class had predicted that the seeds would not germinate in the dark as they knew that plants need light to grow. The great success of this lesson was that the children were happy for their predictions to be wrong. More than happy, they could see what it meant – that they had discovered some new science. They were excited to have learned something new and unexpected.

Introduction

One of the joys of teaching science is that children are often delighted and amazed by what they find out for themselves. Unfortunately, unlike germinating seeds in the dark, many scientific discoveries are elusive and can take professional scientists years of persistent investigation and careful record keeping. A key role of the creative science teacher therefore is to look for ways to guide children in the right direction, while allowing them the freedom to discover the science themselves.

Why do children need to be in the driving seat?

Traditional models of education see the teacher as the font of knowledge and the learners as vessels to be filled. However, constructivist approaches (e.g. Vygotsky, 1978) argue that the learner is more creative, that we build our own learning by comparing new experiences or ideas with previous ones and asking whether they make sense. Does the new learning fit with the picture of the world that has been built up over the years? If not then it is very likely that the new idea will not be taken on as truth. As a concept, the idea that seeds can germinate in the dark will be compared to previously held knowledge about plants and where they grow, to see how it fits. As plants are usually found outside, on window sills and in other light places such as greenhouses it is a logical step to ignore this new concept as nonsense. But as an activity, for children to find it out by practical investigation and to see it for themselves, it provides them with a new and memorable experience. In this case, it is far more likely to be taken on board as an important new fact to be accommodated into their previous learning. Constructivism therefore seeks an active rather than passive role for the learner.

There is support for the constructivist approach to practical work in science in Geoff Petty's book *Evidence-based Teaching* (Petty, 2009). Evidence from John Hattie's review of educational research (Hattie, *et al.*, 1996) led Petty to propose that one of the main features of any effective classroom strategy is a challenging goal that requires student activity on constructivist methods.

But it is not enough to be 'hands on'. New learning can be strengthened through group or class discussions that link the new idea to previous learning. In our example above, the discussion could reflect on a time when the children planted seeds in soil and covered them up. Children could explore their own ideas about what it is like underground in caves and down tunnels, and also perhaps about moles and earthworms and their lack of sight. These relevant and linked ideas will allow children to understand that seeds almost always germinate in the dark. So children need to be both hands on and minds on; as creative teachers we can help children make the cognitive links that will embed the new idea within a web of understanding in the brain.

Giving children an increasingly active and autonomous role in learning science leads to greater engagement, which in turn assists their understanding of science questions, of the design of investigations and of the limitations of evidence. Encouraging children to take more responsibility also requires them to practise the skills needed to become completely independent learners. A simple class exploration of 'What do you know?' and 'What do you want to know?' begins a powerful metacognitive process that can be strengthened post-task by reflecting on 'What have you learned?'

For a teacher seeking creativity this is the ideal approach as it can be used to encourage imaginative and purposeful activity that can lead to new discoveries and ideas. This way of working is effective but also motivating for the children. Many children enjoy practical tasks for their own sake but even more so when these are purposeful and creative, in this case creating their own knowledge.

Creative teaching that develops independent learning

How then do we put children in the driving seat? As teachers, there are things we can do to shift responsibility to the children. We could call this creative teaching. But there are also attitudes and approaches to learning we would like the children to develop. This is our creative learning.

In the rest of this chapter we consider approaches to creative teaching that develop independent learning.

Teaching the scientific process: it's not just fair testing!

In order for children to be able to take more control of their learning in science they need to become involved in the complete scientific process, from asking the initial question, to planning, carrying out the enquiry and presenting the results. So what does this complete process look like? It falls neatly into three sections: exploration and question raising, collecting evidence through enquiry, and making conclusions (Table 3.1).

Table 3.1 The scientific process

Exploration and questioning	To explore an idea, statement, question, problem, artefact or living thing then ask a question based on the exploration
Scientific enquiry to collect evidence	• Observing changes over time • Identifying and classifying • Pattern seeking • Research (using secondary sources) • Fair testing
Making conclusions	To answer the question, solve the problem, develop an explanation or evaluate an artefact or system, providing evidence to justify the conclusion and/or to ask more questions

Source: adapted from Turner (2012).

The scientific process can be considered to be a cycle. It is common for children to ask further questions during the process, which then in turn create further enquiries.

Concern that many teachers were concentrating solely on fair testing as a method of scientific enquiry led to a broader approach in the National Curriculum (DfE, 2013), which emphasizes that scientific questions should be addressed using different types of enquiry. The different methods of enquiry in Table 3.1 will be familiar to more experienced teachers and we will not go into detail about them here. However, the box below gives an example of how identifying and classifying can be used creatively to develop children's thinking.

With appropriate support and differentiation children in all year groups across the school can use the five types of scientific enquiry listed in Table 3.1. There should be progression in terms of the complexity of the activity and the level of autonomy, including the degree to which they are involved in the planning. So at Key Stage 1 there may be a whole-class discussion about what seasonal changes they should look out for over the course of a year. At lower Key Stage 2 there might be a degree of choice in adapting an enquiry question about patterns in human growth. Do older children have longer legs, or bigger hands? Do taller children have bigger feet, or longer arms? At upper Key Stage 2 we would hope that children would become familiar with planning all five types of enquiry so that they are able to make creative choices about which methods are most suitable to answer their questions. Children need opportunities to apply these skills in a variety of contexts as each one will use the skills in a slightly different way and make links with different areas of understanding in the brain. There is more on supporting children in planning science enquiry in Chapter 11.

Developing creative thinking through identification and classification

Sorting is an activity that requires children to apply their identification and classification skills but it also develops observational skills. Presented with a group of objects to sort and the freedom to create their own groups, many children will begin by choosing the most obvious characteristic that some of the objects have in common and put them into one group. For example, when sorting a collection of rocks they may identify three larger rocks and put them together. Commonly, the next step is to look at the remaining objects and to again identify the most obvious characteristic as the classification for the next group – e.g. these four rocks are all black. This continues until all the objects are in groups but it is obviously neither a scientific nor a helpful way to go about things. The children may well end up with a black rock that is not in the group of black rocks because it is large and was put into a group before the group of black rocks was even thought of. This is a complicated thinking process and trying to explain it to children so that they avoid the mistake will end up leaving everyone confused. So give them the freedom to do it and let them make this mistake because then it is easy to explain. 'But why is this black rock not in the black rock group?' you can ask. 'Because it's a large rock,' they might reply, and when you say 'But it's also black,' now they should see that there is a problem. Then you can help them solve the problem by choosing a criterion for their sorting before they start and sticking with it. Of course, with encouragement and the freedom to experiment the children may create this solution for themselves. This can be as simple as choosing 'size' and putting the rocks into two groups: large and small. The next step is to increase the number of groups: small, medium and large. This could be repeated until you have a continuous line. 'We have sorted the rocks from smallest to largest', or from roughest to smoothest, darkest to lightest. This is called a continuum. When you think about it, the same thing occurs across science;

separate colours blend into a rainbow; babies, children and adults blend into the continuum of age. Often the classifications are only really there for our convenience – they simplify a complex world. When does a teenager become an adult? When does spring become summer?

This is all sorting using a single criterion. Introducing two criteria gets even more exciting. Too many criteria is exactly what was going wrong before, but introducing them carefully can lead to useful discoveries. Ask children to sort a selection of coloured pencils into two groups: long ones and red ones. The children are now faced with the same problem we had before with the large, but black, rock. However, this time there are only two groups to choose from and they have a long red pencil to put somewhere. Generally they will place it in the middle, between the two groups. If each group is on a separate piece of paper they may well overlap the two pieces thus following the footsteps of the philosopher John Venn and inventing, for themselves, the Venn diagram.

All these identification and classification activities involve plenty of talking, listening, agreeing and disagreeing, and allow for both peer assessment and assessment for learning by the teacher.

Creative planning to encourage curiosity

Children will readily take responsibility for their own learning when they feel engaged and motivated. As teachers, then, we should plan to engage children's curiosity and allow a series of lessons to be driven by their questions. While there is always a logical forward progression of ideas and understanding within a science topic, curiosity often runs in the opposite direction. For example, an upper Key Stage 2 topic on plant life cycles may be planned to logically follow the cycle from seed to plant to flower to fruit and then seed again. But to teach in this order somehow goes against the grain of curiosity. The children's responses at the end of each section are likely to be straightforward (see Table 3.2).

Table 3.2 Example topic: plant life cycles (a)

Step	Content	Children's response
1	Some seeds grow into plants with flowers	We know
2	The flowers are pollinated so they can grow seeds to reproduce	OK, this makes sense
3	The seeds grow inside a fleshy fruit or special pod that helps them to be dispersed	Yes, I see

But now, look what can happen if you take a more creative approach and teach it 'backwards' so that you start with seed dispersal (see Table 3.3).

Table 3.3 Example topic: plant life cycles (b)

Step	Content	Children's response
1	What is inside these fruits and pods?	Are these seeds? Why are they inside fruit? How did they get there?
2	The fruits and pods used to be flowers	But why, how have they changed?
3	The flowers are pollinated, which allows them to grow seeds	So flowers allow plants to make seeds

By presenting children with a series of puzzles to be solved, rather than a sequence of facts to be learned, their curiosity is engaged. The children are motivated because the development of the lessons is naturally following their questions.

Let us take electricity as another example. The topic may well be planned to follow a logical sequence of ideas; exploring static electricity, knowing that electricity comes from batteries or the mains, knowing that electricity flows in wires then lighting a bulb in a circuit. But, again, teaching it backwards allows for a natural flow of questions.

Table 3.4 Example topic: static electricity

Step	Content	Children's response
1	Can you get this bulb to light up in a circuit?	Yes. Why does it light up? How does it work? Why is it hot?
2	Look at the bulb closely with a magnifying glass	The little wire goes orange then white. It's getting hot and glowing. But why?
3	Electricity is flowing inside the wires; the battery pushes it around	What is electricity? What's moving? Will it only move in metal wires?

Challenging children's misconceptions

Another creative teaching strategy is to plan activities that are likely to challenge children's misconceptions. For example, one commonly held misconception is that materials that keep warm things warm, like thick coats or woolly hats, will also make cold things warmer. So encourage children to investigate which materials are best at keeping warm water warm. At this stage it is important to ask the children to compare a material that they think will work well with one that they think will do badly. The results will probably match the children's predictions. So then encourage them to ask how they can keep cold water cold and repeat the experiment with the same selection of materials, again choosing one that they think will work well and one they think will do badly. Now they are likely to find their predictions are incorrect but that they have learned something new as the same material works well in both cases. This is a productive way of working so long as the atmosphere in the classroom is one that values new learning over being correct and the children are aware that a good prediction is one that is made using logic and experience. A good prediction that turns out to be wrong makes new learning clearly visible.

Another example of this can be seen in a lesson on filtering, where the children mixed different solids such as sand and salt with water and then separated them by filtering. The children quickly found that solids that dissolve cannot be removed by filtering and, having discovered this for themselves, are more likely to remember it.

Teachers as questioners

For children to discover things for themselves the teacher's role has to switch from the giver of information to the asker of questions. Petty calls this 'teaching by asking' (Petty, 2009). He argues that it is the natural instinct of curiosity in all animals that leads us to learn. Sometimes all that curiosity needs is a questioning spark to get it going. However, the way our questions are constructed can have a considerable impact on the attitude of the learner. For example, with a group of children whose investigation is not working, the question 'What's going wrong?' will be received very differently from 'Can you explain the problem?' or 'Which parts are working?'

Open questions with a multitude of answers will always provide more routes to success than closed questions and they encourage children to be more creative with their responses. Rhetorical questions, too, can be very powerful, particularly the 'I wonder . . .' kind as they tend to be infectious. Even 'I wonder how long it is until dinner?' is hard to ignore! The 'I wonder wall' (Figure 3.1) makes an effective focus for a display as well as a stimulus for children's questions.

In order to encourage creativity in children's responses, give them thinking time or, even better, time to discuss in pairs or small groups, before attempting answers. Encourage children to explain their thinking and to question one another's responses.

Figure 3.1 I wonder wall

An important principle for child-led learning is that if the children are to be 'hands on', then teachers and teaching assistants need to be 'hands off' as much as possible (Feasey, 2007). When children are struggling in a practical task, help needs to come in a form that encourages them to think about what to change about what they are doing or how to improve it. Carefully constructed guiding questions are likely to be more effective in terms of learning than simply demonstrating the correct method.

> **Teaching Tip**
>
> Teach by asking questions.

Making it manageable

It takes time and practice to get used to having more control in practical work. Increasing children's independence can be structured by slowly increasing the number of choices that they make in lessons.

Table 3.5 Giving children choices

Increasing independence	Teacher	Children
	Chooses the investigation	Choose which variables to control or alter
	Chooses the enquiry question	Choose the method of enquiry
	Chooses a science topic	Choose a question and method of enquiry

Creative learning that develops autonomy

A key aim of creative primary science teaching is to develop autonomy in learners who, with their developing knowledge and understanding, can use their skills independently. We will now consider a range of techniques that encourage creative and autonomous learning.

Teaching idea: Elicitation

A great way to initiate the learning process is to run an elicitation activity. Elicitation serves two purposes. The first is assessment for learning – elicitation lets you know what the children know. This allows you to adjust your lesson plan accordingly. Asking children to work on an activity designed to demonstrate that mirrors are not a light source is fairly wasteful of time if they already have a good understanding of why they

Figure 3.2 Children sorting their ideas using sticky notes

are not! The second outcome of elicitation is that it helps the children work out for themselves what they know and what they don't know, thus starting the process of metacognition by requiring them to assess their own understanding. This is a key part of the creative process as it allows children to evaluate their progress.

There are many good elicitation techniques and the best include a strong element of discussion. All elicitation activities benefit from time spent on open-ended practical exploration as preparation for the elicitation itself. For example, given a couple of minutes using torches, mirrors, lenses and colour filters, children will find it much easier to remember previous experiences both in and out of school to do with light. Along with a discussion about previous learning in the topic, this will focus children on the topic to be taught and allow them to recall more easily what they already know and any questions they may have.

One particularly useful technique is to ask children to record what they know on sticky notes, one fact per note; these can then be collected together and moved around. They can be sorted into the beginnings of a structure that frames the topic. Children's questions can also be recorded on to sticky notes of a different colour and added to the structure. In this way we can create a community of enquiry, mapping what is already known and what the community would like to find out. In many ways this is similar to how the scientific research community works (Lunn, 2006).

Teaching idea: Asking questions

Asking questions is the basis of science. If scientists asked no questions there would be no scientific process. Questioning is a specified skill within the National Curriculum

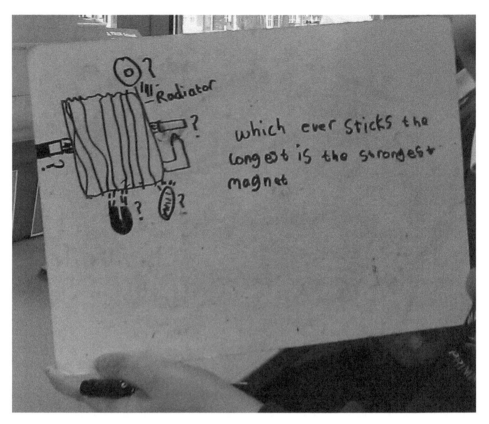

Figure 3.3 The 'wrong' question! A child proudly displays the group's planning

(DfE, 2013) and, like the other skills required to work scientifically, asking questions is something that children need to develop and practise. As a teacher, your own questions will model this skill, but children need plenty of opportunity to ask their own questions. Questions often stimulate discussion and children can ask one another, ask the teacher and develop more formal questions as part of the scientific process.

Like many poems, a question is usually constructed from only a few words and the words chosen make a great difference to its meaning. Children need to be encouraged to see these differences and use their words carefully. The question 'Which magnet is the strongest?' provides a good example of how the wording of a question can cause confusion. In planning for this investigation with a Year 3 class it became clear that the children were using different interpretations of 'strongest'. Two alternative measures of strength, as seen on the television programme *The World's Strongest Man*, are the weight of the object that can be lifted and the length of time for which an object can be held. Some children were planning to test the strength of the magnets by attaching them to a vertical metal surface and seeing how long they could stay on before they got tired! Changing the question to 'Which magnet has the strongest pull?' clarified the meaning of 'strongest'.

There is information in Chapter 11 on helping children to structure questions using a question matrix.

Teaching idea: What about 'difficult' questions?

Many teachers are concerned about children's questions that they are not able to answer. However, we would argue that such questions should be praised and encouraged. An unanswered question is an opportunity to research or investigate, but it is also a chance for teachers to demonstrate their own love of learning. 'What a great question. I don't know. I wonder if it is to do with . . . I can't wait to find out.' Such responses will motivate children to want to do their own research, while praising the asker and demonstrating that questioning and learning are highly valued in the classroom. A display of 'great unanswered questions' is an engaging feature for any classroom. It could be an interactive feature, perhaps with questions written on sticky notes, but with some facility for the children to also post answers they have discovered.

Teaching idea: Generating questions through observation

Observing leads naturally to questioning; as children begin to notice details, differences and similarities in the things they are observing the questions become obvious. Why do the snail's eye stalks move in and out like that? Why do snails leave a trail of slime? Why is the Moon up now in the daytime? Observation, then, is a good way to start a topic or a lesson as it will motivate children to want to find out more.

Art

Teacher questioning is important during observation as children can be directed towards details that might otherwise be missed. Which is your favourite snail and why? Asking children to choose and justify a favourite is a particularly useful question when discussed as a group as it requires a creative response that is both emotional and contains some observation of detail. There is plenty of opportunity for cross-curricular work with art here. Observational drawing activities will contribute greatly to children's observational skills.

Talking scientifically

Within the National Curriculum 2014, working scientifically includes:

- asking questions
- making predictions
- identifying differences, similarities and changes
- explaining findings
- considering the degree of trust in results
- using results to suggest answers.

All of these skills can be developed through talk between pupils. Sometimes this can be informal, part of a practical investigation maybe, but it can also be more structured as part of a whole-class discussion or group presentation.

Teaching idea: Encouraging discussion

Vygotsky (1978) proposed a 'zone of proximal development' to describe the things a learner can do with help but not on their own. This goes some way to explaining why children often achieve more when working with others. Discussion in pairs or groups allows children to consider the ideas of others and to learn from other people's successes or mistakes as well as their own. Of course, the more the children are talking, the more the teacher can listen, thus providing plenty of opportunity for assessment for learning.

The elicitation activities above are just one way to get children to talk and share ideas. Organizing talking partners is another. Asking children to consult a partner to discuss a question before answering is an inclusive technique that many creative teachers use. It encourages participation and almost always results in more and better contributions. It encourages the sharing of children's ideas and thus encourages creativity. In some classrooms the strategy is very structured and involves seating plans and a rota of different partners across the year, but it can also work informally as 'talk to the person next to you'.

Children can be taught to use the phrases 'I agree' and 'I disagree' with each other as they show more respect for the opinions of others than saying 'You're wrong, Natasha is right.' Everyone can be included in discussions by asking children to put up hands to show whether they agree or disagree with one pupil's prediction or statement. Individuals can be asked to explain why they agree or disagree, thus shaping the discussion and modelling the more complex thinking skills of analysis and evaluation.

Another approach for developing discussion skills is to use Kagan structures (Kagan, 1990). These are simple organizational methods that enable children to discuss and work effectively in groups. Many involve taking turns to speak and encourage listening by asking children to give feedback on what they have heard. For example in the Timed Pair Share activity, children talk for a set time while their partner listens then summarizes what was said. The pair then swap roles.

There is more information on Kagan structures here:

www.kaganonline.com/free_articles/research_and_rationale/330/The-Essential-5-A-Starting-Point-for-Kagan-Cooperative-Learning (tinyurl.com/lfqpabc)

Teaching idea: Explaining by talking

Explanations are a particularly powerful talking point. Have you ever felt that you understood something only to discover, when you tried to explain it to someone else, that your knowledge was less secure than you thought? Creating a verbal explanation is a particularly good way to reinforce understanding; Keith Ross calls the process reformulation (Ross, 2013). Children can be encouraged to be creative in their explanations of science ideas by displaying key words or a summary of key points on the board, or by asking older children to prepare rough notes about what they want to say. For most of us, talking is easier than writing so children will benefit from time spent developing their explanations orally before trying to write them down. This approach can also be effective for other written science, such as questions, predictions and conclusions.

This technique is useful across the curriculum and has been developed into a well-known literacy scheme called Talk for Writing by Pie Corbett. See:

www.talk4writing.co.uk (tinyurl.com/q9glp47)

Conclusion

In order to work scientifically in an effective and creative way, children need to be aware of the scientific process and how the creative choices that they are able to make contribute to it. The scientific process is a creative one from beginning to end and, when children are involved in it – from coming up with the question to presenting the conclusions – they will be able to see the value and purpose of their work and how it contributes to their learning.

Chapter summary

- Giving children increased control in practical work is supported by the constructivist theory of learning.

- Children's thinking can be developed by asking them to explain and justify their decisions.

- Getting children talking and questioning supports creative science.

4

ICT and computing

What will you learn from this chapter?

- How ICT and computing can contribute to creative science.
- About the vast range of applications and contexts in which ICT and computing can be used.
- That you need to be very selective in order to ensure that science and creativity are enhanced by the use of ICT and computing.

Is a computer like a pencil? One teacher explained her view that, like a pencil, a computer is dead without human creativity. At the fingertips of a person with an active mind, both pencil and computer can create and develop stories, lives, images, investigations, research, calculations and much, much more. The most complex tool created by humankind, the computer still requires our input to enable its incredible functionality. Our schoolchildren are learning in a world increasingly dominated by computers, and their working and personal lives will be strongly influenced by their interaction with computers. As a society our interaction with computers will influence our present and all our futures. All scientists use computers to do the science, deal with results and communicate their findings. As teachers we owe it to our pupils to explore the full potential of every new facility offered by computers.

QR codes

A class are asked to take a tour of the school site observing trees on the site. At the base of a number of trees is a board with a QR (quick response) code, which the children use to access information about that tree.

Living
Things

One of the codes takes the children to a blank page of the class blog asking for content about this tree.

Figure 4.1 QR code for http://www.woodlandtrust.org.uk/learn/british-trees/native-trees/english-oak/

We should of course consider a word of warning as computers and the internet offer such a wealth of resources we can be fooled into thinking that they can teach science. Computers offer a great enhancement and enrichment to science and science education, but they cannot provide the practical hands-on engagement with real materials, phenomena and a capable teacher that are so important to young learners. Children should be warned about the danger of accepting everything online as the truth, as anyone can post anything online. The helpful example of the Pacific Northwest Tree Octopus is referred to in Chapter 5.

The English National Curriculum (DfE, 2013) includes the subject of computing, which is about the ways we instruct computers to do what we want. In the other primary subjects there is reference to ICT (information and communication technology), which is a broader reference to the many ways we use ICT to achieve our aims, including communication. In this book we argue that learners need to be put in charge of science investigations, and ICT applications and resources can enable this shift. ICT resources have a strong capacity to provide motivation, partly through the wealth of resources and applications available, e.g. communicating with others around the world via blogs and QuadBlogging (see below).

Computing

As primary teachers we have to teach computing across all subjects, and specifically the subject of computing as set out in the 2014 National Curriculum (DfE, 2013). Computing in the English National Curriculum is divided into three aspects:

1. computer science
2. IT
3. digital literacy.

These are defined as follows:

The core of computing is **computer science**, in which pupils are taught the principles of information and computation, how digital systems work and how to put this knowledge to use through programming. Building on this knowledge and understanding, pupils are equipped to use **information technology** to create **programs**, systems and a range of content. Computing also ensures that pupils become **digitally literate** – able to use, and express themselves and develop their ideas through, information and communication technology – at a level suitable for the future workplace and as active participants in a digital world.

(Computing at School, 2013: 5)

Thus in computer science learners are expected to learn to control computers using systems of codes or programming language (Computing at School, 2013). These codes include sets of instructions or numerical algorithms. While in primary science lessons we might not learn about coding, we can use IT, e.g. a database where children add data, and select fields and parameters within the database or a blog or app, where children write about their science. These are areas for strong creativity as learners are expected to use computers in a similar way to a pencil and paper. These open-content IT environments offer great scope for creativity. For example, an empty page on a word processor says nothing, however type on it a question such as

What is the best material to make sunglasses?

and things can begin – in this case science.

In addition to curriculum changes, the world of computing itself is and will continue to keep changing rapidly. Schools are replacing ICT suites with sets of laptops and class sets of tablet computers. Wi-fi in schools is now commonplace and reliable. The Cloud offers seemingly limitless resources and storage. This is leading to an explosion of materials in app-type applications:

---

http://www.cc-apps.co.uk/page/109/Science.htm – an app which supports the teaching of primary science (Cross, 2012).

---

and in communication and image creation.

Computers and learners' science

Computers can help children learn science. From a humble hand-held digital camera (see Chapter 7) or decibel meter to tablet computers, laptops and desktop computers, there are options that enable and enhance science and science education.

Initially learners may need to research a topic to find out more about the science, e.g. shadows or microorganisms. Teachers can approach this in different ways, but putting the learners in the position of 'expert' or researcher with a challenge or question to answer can give them more responsibility. With sufficient child protection measures, electronic resources on the internet allow learners to research aspects of the world, including science. Learners will use search engines at home, some with little supervision, so this is a great opportunity to have them learn to protect themselves and search efficiently.

As a teacher you need to scaffold this research with support regarding questions that might be posed. Is it clear why we are looking for information? Is it clear who the information is for? Can we prompt ways in which questions can be posed scientifically, perhaps using words such as how, why and when? What key words will trigger useful information? Can we check that we are looking for science? Where is the creativity here? Is it in the original question posed? In the scope of research? In the presentation of results? In the use of the information to develop and create new approaches?

Computing encourages children to work together collaboratively on projects, including investigations. Groups that are encouraged to be creative will almost always generate more ideas and possible ways forward.

Computing can assist greatly with measurement in primary science as it includes the low-maintenance hand-held sound and other sensors, which don't connect to a computer, and the more sophisticated dataloggers, which enable all sorts of ways to view, record and handle data collected in science experiments.

Learners can begin to feel more like scientists when they handle specialized equipment and sets of data they have collected. This equipment can help to shift control towards the children as they can easily gather accurate data quickly, giving them more time to discuss results.

Sound

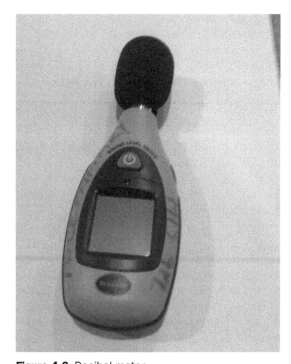

Figure 4.2 Decibel meter

Source: Alan Cross

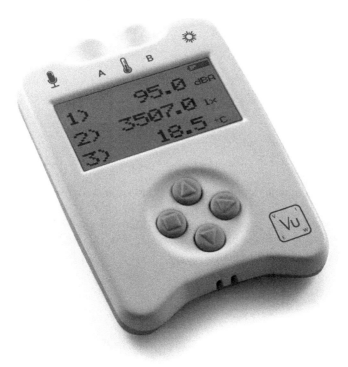

Figure 4.3 The Data Harvest Vu datalogger

The datalogger will give real-time readings of temperature, light intensity and sound levels, as well as taking snapshots and recording results in real time – for example, taking a temperature reading every 5 seconds over a period of half an hour. This is exactly the kind of equipment used by scientists as it is accurate and reliable, and can take many more readings than even a skilled technician.

Light, Heat and Sound

A datalogger is a true 'open content' device in that it requires to be set up in an experiment, test or observation in order to gather data, which can then be interpreted. The set-up includes the other science equipment and resources but also choices within the menu of the datalogger – for example, how often will the datalogger take a reading? Every second? Ten seconds? Or every minute or hour? Dataloggers require real understanding of the investigation, and so they encourage thought and decision making by the learners.

Dataloggers and spreadsheets offer perhaps the strongest links between primary science and the subject of computing (DfE, 2013). Learners can at the simplest level use the datalogger in real time as a sensor just like any other thermometer, decibel meter or light meter. Dataloggers can also be set up to record either or all light, sound and temperature. The settings can be adjusted to gather data at different intervals and over different periods of time. While this is not in itself coding, it is an opportunity for learners to control variables and use the power of microprocessing to achieve their particular objective, e.g. recording the temperature in the classroom every minute for 24 hours. The resulting spreadsheets can themselves be used to then sift and sort data.

Maths

Teaching idea: Handling data

Presenting and handling data makes a significant contribution to primary science. Using packages such as Pictogram and Datasweet:

> http://www.kudlian.net/products/

children can simply type in data from tests and instantly see a useful graph drawn for them on screen.

This very professional presentation of data allows learners to read graphs more easily and also to gain a sense of professionalism. This can add to confidence and a child's willingness to try new approaches.

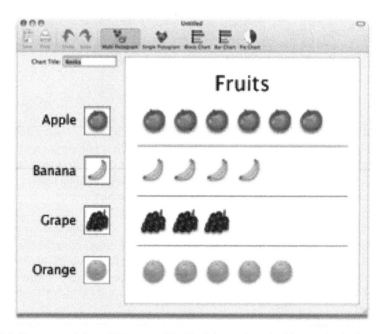

Maths

Figure 4.4 Screen shot from Pictogram (Kudlian) (reproduced with permission)

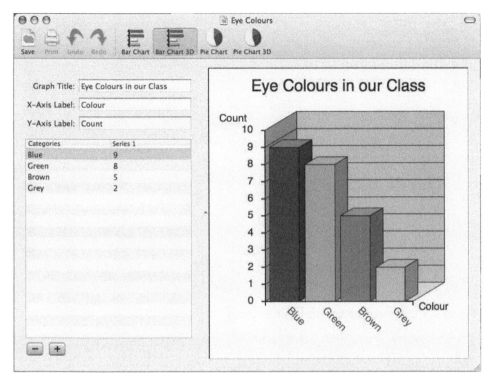

Figure 4.5 Screen shot from Datasweet (Kudlian) (reproduced with permission)

Teaching idea: Written communication

ICT offers all sorts of options for communication. From word processors to Twitter via email and Skype, IT provides options for children to communicate with one another and to a wider audience.

English

One school that has made significant use of blogging by the children has experienced a measurable improvement in writing, particularly among boys. One child described the delight of having a real audience: 'You know that someone on the other half of the world is liking your work and you feel like you've travelled there.'

Contact a colleague or friend at another school and arrange for communication between the classes by email, QuadBlogging or Skype (see below). Learners can share topics, questions and investigations – in fact, any aspect of science.

Online collaborative applications mean that learners can share ideas – for example, Bubbl.us allows us to ask questions and to be inspired by the questions of others. Learners can soon see that the contributions of others assist them in developing ideas.

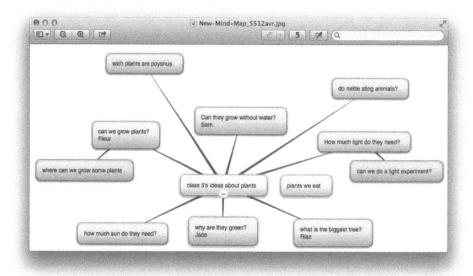

Figure 4.6 Class ideas about plants on Bubbl.us

Teaching idea: Audio, still and video recording

Audio, still and video recording tend to increase learners' ownership of science and can encourage creativity. A learner in a group can be given the task of recording stages in an investigation, which can help with the presentation and review of results. A simple audio recorder or the same facility on a computer will allow learners to record their thoughts as they work and/or their results and conclusions as they move through an investigation or activity. A simple online resource such as audioboo.com allows these simple recordings to be stored and shared online.

Art and Design

Teaching idea: Graphics

Drawing on the computer offers another way for learners to express ideas about science. Free online tools such as:

http://www.onemotion.com/flash/sketch-paint/

offer a straightforward set of drawing tools.

Teaching idea: Visualizers and computer microscopes

The world of the small and very small is one that can fill us all with awe when we see the detail of materials and objects that our unaided eye cannot see. A classroom visualizer or computer microscope allows children and teachers to present a range of materials and resources, and to film and take photographs of these. Seeing aspects of the world in a different way encourages thinking differently about the world.

Teaching idea: Websites

There is now a wealth of websites available to help your planning and delivery of primary science. Perhaps most useful are portal sites such as the author's:

http://www.jbprimaryscience.co.uk/

This links you to a considerable range of high-quality resources and sites. Learners need to be encouraged to engage with the material and to think about ways the ideas can be used, ways that are perhaps new to them.

Teaching idea: Apps

Almost all of us are aware of the ease of use and access of a well-designed smartphone or tablet app. As some children have these at home you may want to recommend science apps. All teachers would, we feel, want to use such apps alongside the many beautiful non-fiction books available. Where schools have available smartphones or tablet computers these science apps may be of interest. They may stimulate interest, encouraging children to develop a real personal enthusiasm.

For instance, learners could be tasked to research aspects of objects in the night sky, and predict the movement of the Sun, Moon and planets in the coming hours. They might be asked to design and write additional pages of information or indeed their own app about an object in space.

Earth in Space

Other free primary science apps worth considering include those listed on pages 48–49.

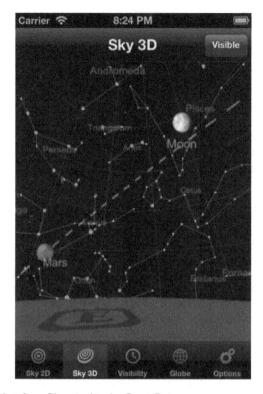

Figure 4.7 Screen shot from Planets App by Dana Peters

For iPhone

- Planets
- Stopwatch
- Measures Lite
- Camera
- Video

For iPad

- Science Lab
- Science Glossary
- Science Facts
- Science Fun
- 1001 Science

- ITrack Wildlife Lite
- Birds Pro HD

For Android

- Science for Kids
- Seasons!
- Kids Science Planets
- Kids Science
- Kids Science Experiments
- Science Dictionary
- Science Experiments

Teaching idea: Skype and videoconferencing

Forms of videoconferencing offer opportunities to speak to specialists remotely and to share our science with others. Some classes routinely communicate with other classes around the world and are able then to talk about all aspects of their lives and work in school, including science. Could they report their findings? Could they share an investigation? Could they gather more data and ideas from the other class?

English

Teaching idea: Blogging and QuadBlogging

Blogs offer the opportunity for an audience and, as such, a powerful way to make writing meaningful. Ideas about science, proposed investigations and investigations can be posted for others to comment on. There are examples of school science blogs, for instance:

> http://pr-science.boltonschool-primary.me
>
> though it is more common for science to feature on class pages within school sites:
>
> http://43p.plymouthgrove.net

These sites allow children, parents and others to see what children have been doing in school. This gives learners a real sense of pride but more importantly of an audience for their work.

Figure 4.8 QuadBlogging website

Source: http://quadblogging.net

English

QuadBlogging provides a quick link between your own and three other schools around the world. Children can then communicate and share ideas about their lives and school work, including science.

Teaching idea: Authoring apps

English

Learners can use simple-to-use Cloud-based resources such as Blippit to create and then write their own personal apps, which can then be published online. Examples can be seen at:

http://www.planetblippit.co.uk/see-apps/

with a science example at:

http://www.planetblippit.co.uk/view-app/?appid=6600

This sort of presentation may be quite new to learners. They will have to be creative when they think about how the user will access the materials, e.g. text has to be condensed very carefully.

Teaching idea: Interactive whiteboard

As a teacher you may be used to using a computer projector in the classroom and, with it, perhaps an interactive whiteboard. These resources have revolutionized some of what happens in schools. In science they allow us a window on the world and much more. At times however they are used simply as an electronic chalkboard. How can we use interactive whiteboards more creatively in science? The following questions may assist.

- Who uses the IWB/projector most? Is it you or the children? Could you shift the emphasis towards the children? Can they take charge? Can they be the teachers?
- Are you making use of open-content applications like word processors, audio recorders, app writers etc., which enable learners to input their own ideas and data?

Teaching idea: Quick response (QR) codes

QR codes can be linked to science sites so that any 'smart' device with a QR reader can quickly access more information via the site. The codes can be made very easily by yourself or the children at free sites such as:

http://www.qrstuff.com

just have your target website's URL ready.

Learners might create a science display with their own research and work relating to rocks, QR codes might take you to the class blog, or specific websites and pages about rocks.

Teaching idea: Google Earth and webcams

Google Earth offers unparalleled access to view landscapes and habitats from above and, in some cases, with Street View. There is also access to up-to-date and detailed imagery from the Moon and from Mars. Can learners research sites, habitats and features like the North and South Poles of Earth? Can children write a visitors' guide to Earth?

Geography

Figure 4.9 QR code for http://www.childrensuniversity.manchester.ac.uk

Even more detail can be found from various websites, including webcams from around the world. Webcams are now available all over the Earth. They can tell you about habitats, and whether it is day or night on the other side of the planet. The following examples give some indication of the power of these resources.

Hong Kong:

http://www.hko.gov.hk/wxinfo/ts/webcam/HKO_e_realtime.htm

Live view of Mont Blanc:

http://www.savoie-mont-blanc.com/en/Live/Webcams?gclid=CKbp8MGIursCFU kCwwodPQQAOg

Live from Palm Beach, Florida:

http://www.earthcam.com/search/ft_search.php?term=Palm+Desert%2C+ California

Yellowstone National Park:

http://volcanoes.usgs.gov/volcanoes/yellowstone/yellowstone_multimedia_10. html

Volcano – Popocatepetl, Mexico:

http://www.cenapred.unam.mx/popo/UltimaImagenVolcanI.html

UK rivers:

http://www.farsondigitalwatercams.com/live-webcams/

The live day and night map:

http://www.timeanddate.com/worldclock/sunearth.html

shows viewers exactly where day and night is right now all over the planet.

Learners can compare familiar features of their local world and compare them with localities and environments around the world. They might be tasked to devise a solution to a problem locally and then consider how this might be applied in a hot or cold desert area.

Conclusion

Teachers and children now have easy access to a vast range of information and resources. There is far more then you could ever hope to even look at, never mind use. As teachers we therefore need to be very selective and keep our learning objectives clearly in mind. The power of ICT and computers for creativity is manifested in a number of ways:

- in the capacity to inspire and motivate
- in the wealth of sources and applications
- in the way that we do things differently
- in the way we are encouraged to communicate differently.

Computers and ICT by no means offer a guarantee of creativity or indeed quality, but they do provide an opportunity for inspiration, use of information and collaboration, which is perhaps unparalleled in our history. As teachers we have to take the best of these ideas and explore them for their educational worth.

Chapter summary

- Computing and ICT offer science opportunities for creativity.
- It is the user and not the computer that can be creative.
- ICT enables creative use of communication, image use, measuring, and data capture and use.

5

Using children's literature, stories, poetry and songs

What will you learn from this chapter?

- The importance of the link with English and literacy.

- About the potential for stories, poetry and songs in science.

- A range of examples for use in science lessons.

The great strength of effective primary education is the way teachers make learning meaningful. They typically begin from established skills and known contexts and phenomena before moving to new skills, knowledge and understanding. Stories, songs and poems offer a great context and vehicle for presenting science ideas and for initiating science, including science questions. These can be used in science lessons or in linked English or literacy lessons, perhaps as part of a cross-curricular theme.

Do you remember hearing about Archimedes in the bathtub? On pain of death he is said to have puzzled over a way to measure the quantity of gold in the king's crown without damaging the crown. Why do we all remember this so easily, so clearly? Because he cried 'Eureka!' when he worked out that the water displaced by the crown would equal the volume of the gold. People now refer to a 'Eureka moment' when an idea is formulated. As humans we have evolved in an oral culture. We love and remember stories. Our use of number, for example, came much later in our evolution and thus we are often more comfortable dealing with stories of our lives, those of others and of the world around us (Pinker, 1999).

English

Primary teachers know the power of stories, songs and poetry in the classroom, but their full potential might not be used in some subjects, such as science. The history of science is of course itself an intriguing story. Stories of how people invented and discovered things fascinate us. This chapter will refer to a number of these. Stories, songs and verse offer a fun and very inclusive route into thinking about science ideas.

Most learners love to hear tricks and rhythm in language; these all make things memorable and are therefore useful in education.

This chapter makes very obvious links to English and literacy. Of course all science uses language to articulate and describe thoughts, ideas, findings and observations, so in a way every science lesson is a literacy lesson. The learning of each subject can benefit from the other. Science can provide highly engaging contexts for literacy lessons and, of course, increasingly literate learners can make even more of science lessons.

Being creative with stories means that we can add new parts to existing stories, write new stories, learn science from stories, or add to stories with scientific content or illustrations. So what can a story provide for us as teachers of primary science? They illustrate and motivate, they can provide a meaningful context. Children can empathize with characters, they can perceive the needs of characters in a story – real or imaginary. They can perceive a problem, propose a solution, trial a solution and return to the context of the story to suggest a conclusion.

> **Teaching Tip**
>
> Use the power of a story to give your science topic a meaningful and playful context.

Teaching idea: Fictional stories

Children's stories can offer an excellent way to engage children in thinking about elements of primary science. A classic example is the fable of the Three Little Pigs and their need for a house that can survive high wind speeds. This can be a very open-ended play activity or could be treated very scientifically, trialling numerous materials, and methods of construction and house design. Learners can build model houses to illustrate the story; they can then test those models with moving air or force meters. They can conduct tests on materials, constructions, walls with and without foundations, e.g. built in sand trays.

Other classic fairy tales similarly offer a range of possibilities for the creative teaching and learning of primary science:

* Three Little Pigs – *materials, forces*
* The Three Bears – *materials, thermal insulation, nutrition*
* Red Riding Hood – *camouflage, materials*
* Rapunzel – *materials*
* Cinderella – *materials, light, animals*
* The Gingerbread Man – *materials*
* The Man Who Sold his Shadow – *light and shadows.*

Winnie the Pooh and the Blustery Day

Read this story by A.A. Milne (1926) or watch a clip from the Disney animated adaptation (*Winnie the Pooh and the Blustery Day*, 1968) and you will see a wealth of opportunities to study air resistance, friction, strength of materials and more. In one sequence, Rabbit is carried aloft by a garment acting as a kite. His 'kite' carries him high into the air, illustrating the power of air resistance, and learners can immediately talk about things they have seen blowing in the wind – flags, leaves, umbrellas pulling – and kites they have seen and flown. This would be a great time to have learners talk about examples of wind and air resistance. This discussion could be digitally recorded and broadcast, or form the basis of a presentation from a 'green screen' mountain top.

Lots of principles in science can be illustrated in children's fictional literature with excellent illustrations and often a little humour. The story of Mr Bear's difficulty in finding a quiet place to sleep in *Peace at Last* by Jill Murphy is humorous and endearing. This story gives us the opportunity to talk about sound travelling through materials and about how we might investigate materials suitable to minimize sound, e.g. for ear defenders.

Listen to Rosemary Feasey talking about the importance of stories in science education here:

http://www.pstt.org.uk/ext/cpd/engagement-with-puppets/fiction_merits_approach.asp

To get you started, some more stories that you might find interesting and useful are listed in Table 5.1.

Table 5.1 Stories useful as starting points for discussion

Story	Science	Teaching suggestion
Mrs Wobble the Waitress Allan Ahlberg	forces, materials	Test a range of tray surfaces for friction
The Lighthouse Keeper's Lunch Ronda and David Armitage	materials, forces	Investigate pulleys to transport food over a gap
Funnybones Allan Ahlberg	human body, materials	Reassemble the human skeleton
The Foggy Foggy Forest Nick Sharratt	light, materials	Testing translucent materials

The Jolly Postman Janet and Allan Ahlberg	materials	Test materials for envelopes or mailbags
James and the Giant Peach Roald Dahl	habitats	Study the habitats visited by James
Can't You Sleep, Little Bear? Martin Waddell	light and dark, light sources	Light sources and dark, fear of the dark; observe a range of light sources
The Rainbow Fish Marcus Pfister	colour, light, environment	Research the lives of colourful fish, e.g. camouflage
Dinosaurs and All That Rubbish Michael Foreman	environment	A survey of litter in school
Is a Whale the Biggest Thing There Is? Robert Wells	the scale of space	Research the size of the solar system and its Sun and planets
Flat Stanley Jeff Brown	air resistance	Test different materials or shapes for kite design
The Very Hungry Caterpillar Eric Carle	diet, life cycles	Research life cycles or diet, survey preferences about healthy and treat foods
Handa's Surprise Eileen Browne	variety in animals and plants	Research more animals that might steal Handa's fruit
Peace at Last Jill Murphy	sound	Can you help Mr Bear get to sleep?
Elmer the Elephant David McKee	camouflage	Test different skin patterns to hide in tall grass or bushes
The Snail and the Whale Julia Donaldson and Axel Scheffler	variety of life, habitats	Variety of animals, life and habitats
Dear Zoo Rod Campbell	diversity in animals	Research other animals and their needs in a zoo
The Snowman Raymond Briggs	thermal insulation	Investigate materials suitable to keep things cold
Oscar and the Moth Geoff Waring	movement of the Sun in the sky	The moth teaches a cat that the Sun only *appears* to move

Further ideas for popular children's science books are available on my own and Goodreads' websites:

English

http://www.goodreads.com/shelf/show/childrens-science

https://sites.google.com/site/jbprimaryscience/

Teaching idea: Puppets

Puppets offer another strong medium through which children can gain empathy for characters and individuals; they can view the world from the perspective of the puppet. Does the puppet want to keep warm? Does the puppet need a healthy meal? Children can develop their own stories around the puppets, research science that might help the puppet characters and conduct science investigations to the same end. Simon and colleagues (Simon *et al.*, 2008) have illustrated the potential for puppets to promote talk about science in young children. Their use of puppets, including 'Discovery Dog', is summarized at:

> http://www.millgatehouse.co.uk/research/puppets-puppets-promoting-engagement-and-talk-in-science-research-ongoing

The playful context provided by puppets allows learners to engage with the science in a very meaningful context where ideas can develop.

Teaching idea: Poems and mnemonics

Like stories, poems can offer a context and structure around which learners can use and creatively explore the language of science and science ideas.

English

Poems, particularly short ones, can be remembered and, because of their structure and features such as rhyme, stanza and so on, play to our love of pattern and our playfulness. They help us remember words, phrases and ideas. Many of us resort to mnemonics in order to remember things such as the colours of the rainbow and the names of the planets in the solar system (see box).

> **Mnemonics**
>
> 'Richard of York gave battle in vain' reminds us of the colours of the spectrum (rainbow): red, orange, yellow, green, blue, indigo, violet.
>
> 'My very easy method just speeds up naming planets' reminds us of the order and names of the planets in our solar system: Mercury, Venus, Earth, Mars, Jupiter, Saturn, Uranus, Neptune, Pluto. (Pluto is considered by some to be a dwarf planet.)
>
> 'Mrs Gren' reminds us of the features of life in animals: movement, reproduction, sensitivity, growth, reproduction, excretion, nutrition.

Take the opportunity to review the various forms of poetry and verse, and introduce learners to them – throughout this section you will find examples created by the author. The simpler acrostic and shape poems are often a great starting point for a lively, creative approach and, while we may like poems that rhyme and scan, this is not a formal requirement.

> The Sun is a ball in the sky
> It keeps us warm
> It gives us light
> I love the Sun

Poetry can provides insight, emotion, fun, and a pattern that can be copied or adapted. Poems can be a starting point for investigation – for example, about thermal insulation for Granny in the poem 'Granny' by Spike Milligan, or about a diet for a teddy bear in the poem 'Teddy Bear' by A.A. Milne, available online at:

http://www.familyfriendpoems.com/famous/poem/teddy-bear-by-aa-milne

Haiku

This Japanese poetic form can be a delightful way to express ideas. The form is three lines in a 5, 7 and 5 syllable count, totalling 17 syllables, although flexibility is allowed.

> A river running
> A tail flashes brightly
> A sharp splashing sound

> Leaf fall
> Cloak of white
> Buds

English

> An eagle aloft
> Up it soars and up and up
> Its eye seeks

Acrostic

This is another simple form of poetry that children love. The lack of rules for these poems makes them very accessible to children and lends itself to creativity. The link to topics in science can be very obvious.

Empty space all around
A lonely moon in orbit
Rotating every 24 hours
Tilting at 23 degrees
Home to billions of living things

Lions roar
In hot grassy lands
On every day
Never at night.

nO**c**turnal
shado**W**
f**L**y

English

Shape or concrete poems

Shape or concrete poems might be the most accessible form of all for all children. You can provide an outline like those found here:

http://www.pinterest.com/mchoof/concrete-poems/

English

But a few examples will often make it clear to learners that this is easily a very creative form in which they can quickly create something that really is unique.

Bang!
Suddenly
As hot as the Sun
Rushing lava quickly rises
Gases, smoke and lava steam
A thousand sparks in the black night sky
A leopard turns as the Earth shudders she spies
The volcano's eruption after one thousand years of sleep
Anon

Or this one:

The   sticks and
  path of a   around   stones and
     worm winds   then
                              down
                                a
                              hole.
                        Anon

Try writing a shape poem about the trail of a snail.

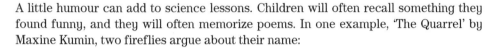

Teaching idea: Humorous verse

Variety of
Life

A little humour can add to science lessons. Children will often recall something they found funny, and they will often memorize poems. In one example, 'The Quarrel' by Maxine Kumin, two fireflies argue about their name:

http://teachers.cpcsc.k12.in.us/jstanley/websites/Audio%20Poems/The%20Quarrel.htm

As well as a starting point for the study of light or invertebrates, learners might rewrite the verse to include other animals with two names, e.g. camel/ship of the desert, cat/feline, lion/leo, perhaps, hog/pig, cattle/cow, borrowing the format from line five onwards.

John Ciardi's poem, 'About the Teeth of Sharks':

http://www.poetryfoundation.org/poem/179965

could easily be the inspiration for a poem about a lion, a tiger, a crocodile or human teeth, as in my example below. References to types of teeth rather than rows could remind learners about incisors, canines, premolars and molars.

About the Teeth of Humans

The thing about my mouth is . . . teeth
Milk teeth above, adult teeth beneath

Now take a closer look. Do you find
Incisors at the front – molars behind?

Still closer here, I'll hold your hat
See that pointy canine tooth, what's behind that?

English

Now look in and . . . Look out! Oh my
You'll never know now! Well, goodbye.

Some verse is just for fun, perhaps adding to playfulness about science. This poem definitely links to the senses. More examples can be found at websites such as these:

http://www.activities-for-the-kids.co.uk/science-poems-for-kids.htm

http://sciencepoems.net

http://www.poetry4kids.com/poem-397.html#.UnNlfRa2P1w

http://www.sciencerhymes.com.au/your-poems

http://www.poetryarchive.org/childrensarchive/singlePoem.do?poemId=16590

English

Limericks convey a great sense of fun, which makes them attractive to learners. Examples of limericks can be found at:

http://grahamlester.webs.com/kids.htm

They are a challenge to write, but selected rhyming words can be changed, initial lines provided as well as whole verses written. Can you finish this one?

Materials exist in three prize states
Solid is one this limerick relates
Liquids are softer and visibly runny
Gases are . . . .
Three states all linked but only one . . . .

Teaching idea: Songs

Songs about science have the added element of the music, which increases the enjoyment and helps us to remember things. The song below about materials is easy to rewrite to suit your own ideas. Of course, for your interest, we should mention Tom Lehrer's famous song 'The Elements':

http://www.privatehand.com/flash/elements.html

This, as well as the one below, illustrates well the fun and opportunity for questions and learning contained in a song.

Glass for Windows (to the tune of *Frère Jacques*)
Glass for windows,
Glass for windows,
It is clear,
It is clear,
So it lets light through,
So it lets light through,
That's why it's here
That's why it's here.

Source: Cross and Bowden (2009)

Materials

Music

Learners could extend this to 'Brick for houses', 'Steel for bridges', 'Wool for jumpers', etc. Are there other familiar tunes we could use? *London Bridge is Falling Down*? Try this one about the water cycle:

Ocean water evaporates, evaporates, evaporates
Ocean water evaporates
And then forms clouds

It rises up condensing more, condensing more, condensing more
It rises up condensing more,
Droplets form as rain

Water Cycle

Could you write a third verse?

Of course songs have been written and published for science:

---

http://www.ks2songs.blogspot.co.uk/2012/11/the-c-ountdown-to-christmas-begins-its.html?m=1#.UngBlL1FBAh

http://www.youtube.com/watch?v=n5cbtptm0qk&list=PLoj4HiBR-4VBLbw0YFmPy-ky3B9F0wbds

http://www.learninggamesforkids.com/science_songs.html

http://www.songsforteaching.com/jennyfixmanedutunes/myheart.htm

---

A very good source of songs is the CD *This is Science* (KS1) by Tim Harding (ISBN 9781855391796), but you can also ask your class to compose their own songs – for example, to the tunes of:

- Baa, Baa, Black Sheep
- If You're Happy and You Know It, Clap Your Hands

- Frère Jacques
- The Wheels on the Bus

Teaching idea: Playscripts

Learners can imagine an interaction between people, objects or phenomena and write a playscript that involves science. For example:

- Magnet 1: My north pole is attracted to your south pole.
- Magnet 2: I need to twist around so my south pole is repelled.
- Magnet 1: We can't move, we're stuck.
- Magnet 2: I wonder if that iron nail can help?
- Magnet 1: Oh no! The nail is attracted to you now and he's stuck too!

Pupils could write short playscripts about the weather, melting, circuits, forces, habitats, working scientifically, materials, life cycles and more.

Teaching idea: Real science stories

Variety of
Life

The stories of real scientists can be very powerful as learning tools. Hearing about Charles Darwin's travels on HMS *Beagle*, how he carefully observed the living things he found and slowly came to the view that the variations he observed – for example, in the shape of beaks in finches living on different islands – were not down to chance. Thus he developed his ideas about evolution by natural selection.

English

> Older children can use websites such as those below. This one has interactive notes on the journey of HMS *Beagle*:
>
> http://www.nhm.ac.uk/nature-online/science-of-natural-history/expeditions-collecting/beagle-voyage/index.html
>
> while the following is an extensive site for children:
>
> http://darwin200.christs.cam.ac.uk/pages/index.php?page_id=j
>
> For adults, there is an amazing collection of Darwin's complete works online at:
>
> http://darwin-online.org.uk

Study of Charles Darwin presents many opportunities as there are still people who deny the proof of evolution, of the science, so there is opportunity to discuss the weight of evidence and the need to take real evidence seriously without denying the right of people to choose to ignore evidence.

Microorganisms

Edward Jenner

Edward Jenner was interested in diseases such as smallpox, and was aware of the folklore that milkmaids who caught the similar but less dangerous disease, cowpox, never contracted smallpox. He famously inserted pus taken from a cowpox pustule into an incision in a boy's arm. The boy suffered the mild cowpox illness but became immune to smallpox. To find out more, see:

http://www.bbc.co.uk/history/historic_figures/jenner_edward.shtml

http://www.jenner.ac.uk/edwardjenner

https://sites.google.com/site/jbprimaryscience/micro-organisms

You might like to consider the following scientists, who are well worth studying:

- Edward Jenner – developed vaccination
- Hypatia – Egyptian mathematician
- Marie Curie – discovered radium
- Dorothy Hodgkin – conformed structure of penicillin
- Drew – founded modern blood banks
- Alexander Fleming – antibiotics
- Galileo – numerous astronomical observations, development of the telescope
- Leonardo da Vinci – numerous inventions, including the steam turbine
- Isaac Newton – numerous discoveries, in maths, the science of light and gravity
- Archimedes – mechanics
- Benjamin Franklin – the lightning rod
- Mary Anning – fossil collector
- Thomas Edison – light bulb
- John Logie Baird – invented a form of television
- Louis Pasteur – pasteurization
- Michael Faraday – discoveries related to electricity
- Alexander Graham Bell – telephone:

http://www.biography.com/people/alexander-graham-bell-9205497

- Barbara McClintock – genetics
- Rachel Carson – marine biologist
- Abbas Ibn Firnas – studied flight
- Al-Battani – astronomer
- Al-Zahrawi – pioneer surgeon
- Ibn al-Nafis – discovered how blood circulates.

Find out more at:

http://www.famousscientists.org

Teaching idea: Children's own stories

English

A story or writing developed by the children is owned by them, and therefore any science developed within that is likely to be meaningful for them. Here are some ideas that you might like to try out (older children can write stories for younger children).

- Can they write a story about a teddy bear who is too cold?
- Could they write about a city overrun by pollution?
- An inspiring story based on true events,

  e.g. the story of the Space Shuttle:

http://www.youtube.com/watch?v=rlG7W0gkjjE

Teaching idea: Secondary sources

Research into the literature is an important part of science and science education. Children need to learn how to find information in books and, of course, to love them for the way they present the world we live in. Can they write a new page for a specific book? Perhaps they could include science facts in a class blog, or contribute articles and pages to a class wiki?

High-quality non-fiction science and other reference books offer a unique resource and an opportunity to develop important research skills and scientific literacy. Because they are published by reputable publishers they offer a more reliable source, but not an infallible one. Learners can learn to use titles, blurbs, summaries, lists of contents, chapters, headings, etc.

One simple approach is to ask the children to write their own non-fiction piece on a topic – for example, the life cycle of the frog. Explain that they are going to write the best ever section of the life cycle. They will do this by researching and reading three or more sources that describe the life cycle. They are tasked to make notes and gather information from the sources. They are then asked to write their own unique account of the life cycle, better than each of the three sources. They should, of course, include a bibliography listing their sources.

Learners need to learn to enjoy and interrogate the wealth of excellent and other material on the internet. Learning to distinguish useful from less useful information and sources, including reliable and less reliable, is very powerful for all learners.

The case of the Pacific Northwest Tree Octopus is a useful tool. This site:

http://zapatopi.net/treeoctopus/

claims to provide information about an endangered tree octopus, but it is entirely fictional. However, the website is presented so professionally that it appears credible. In terms of ICT it offers an example of spurious, unreliable information. In terms of science, learners could consider ways to disprove the existence of the tree octopus – for example, there are no confirming reports or research from other sources.

Figure 5.1 The fictional Pacific Northwest Tree Octopus

Has the advent of the internet led to less use of non-fiction reference books when children in school research science and science-related topics? Use of non-fiction books for research would certainly be included among key skills for life. Science is a fantastic vehicle for literacy. Non-fiction science books often captivate children with excellent pictures, graphics and text.

Conclusion

Stories, songs and poems offer a very rich set of contexts to us as science teachers – they complement science, where language is so very important. Primary teachers know the importance of literacy and English, and so will relish opportunities to bring the subjects together. The familiarity of stories, story formats, and of the patterns in songs and poems, will help to make science more inclusive. This area may also help teachers with their own confidence. Where some teachers might lack confidence in science, most primary teachers are at least reasonably confident in literacy; that confidence and enjoyment should then be infectious in science lessons.

Chapter summary

- Stories can provide a very meaningful context for science.

- Many principles of science are illustrated in stories.

- Use of English can be developed in science classes.

- Pupils can be creative when writing their own stories, songs and poems.

6

Models and analogies

What will you learn from this chapter?

- How and why models and analogies work.
- Creative approaches to using models and analogies.
- Examples of models and analogies.

Models and analogies are an integral part of science. As educators we can use them to make complex things easier to comprehend. Making creative comparisons between things we don't understand and things that we do is a powerful way of making sense of the world around us. Why does the Earth orbit the Sun? A simple explanation can be achieved using the analogy that gravity can pull like a piece of string can pull. A model here can help us: we can picture a piece of string connecting the Earth to the Sun. Imagine whirling a ball on a piece of string around your head and you can begin to understand how gravity stops the Earth from flying off into space.

Analogies are constructed from two concepts that have some similar characteristics; the more characteristics the concepts share, the better the analogy will work. To use analogies as a learning tool, one of the concepts must be familiar, while the other is some part of the new learning. Simply working with analogies requires creative thought (Burrs, 2012) as the two ideas need to be analysed and compared in order to gain understanding about the new concept from the characteristics of the familiar one. However, all analogies fail at some point. The two concepts may be similar in some way but they are not the same. This analogy 'breakdown' happens at the point where the characteristics of the familiar concept are no longer shared with the new idea. It is valuable therefore to encourage children to question and discuss every analogy used to establish explicitly where it breaks down, otherwise it is possible that children will form misconceptions.

When are models and analogies useful?

It is particularly helpful to use models or analogies for concepts that are difficult, abstract, or that are not easy to demonstrate or observe in the classroom. These types of concept fall into three main categories:

1. abstract concepts, such as forces or electricity
2. processes, such as changes of state or the phases of the Moon
3. scale, such as planets in the solar system or how germs spread.

Source: Asoko and de Bóo (2001)

Analogy or model?

An analogy, then, is the theoretical linking of two or more ideas, and is simply a concept. A model, on the other hand, is a recreation of a situation, either in real life, a virtual simulation or in the abstract. A simplified but helpful rule of thumb is that a model represents something by looking like it; an analogy by working like it. A model could be something as simple as recreating the solar system using different-sized pieces of fruit to represent the planets. Or it could be more complex, such as asking children to pretend to be particles of a solid, liquid or gas, and to behave in a particular way to demonstrate the properties of those particles. Scientists working at the forefront of science use complex computer simulations to make predictions by modelling the effects of greenhouse gas emissions, and even economic growth and collapse.

Analogies work like brains work

The understanding of a concept is formed in the brain as a network of connected brain cells or neurons. As our understanding of the idea develops, more and more connections are made to other neuron networks for related concepts. For example, if you were to introduce the word *sphere* to a young child the sound would trigger activity in particular neurons, but in order to understand the concept of what a sphere is the child would need to make links to other related concepts in the brain such as *ball, apple*, etc. As the child's understanding becomes more advanced they will link the concept to the networks of the brain that deal with more abstract concepts such as *circle* and *round*, and then go on to make links to the networks of other 3D shapes: cube, pyramid, etc. So the networks grow and become more interconnected as the concepts become more fully understood and familiar (Petty, 2009).

The more we access any given concept, the stronger the connections in the network become. However, if the neuron network for this concept remains unused because we have not been required to think about it, then the connections between the neurons can become weaker and even fade away completely. This is how we forget. This explains why memory techniques often involve revisiting a topic the next day, the next week and the next month, to ensure that the connections are reused and become stronger.

It is clear to see, then, just why analogies are such a powerful learning tool. They are a device that enables our brains to do what they do best, create meaningful links between new concepts and pre-existing ideas.

It's only a model!

All models and analogies have limitations. We are using a simple concept to help us to understand a more complex one but, by necessity, the two concepts are not the same. At some point the analogy will break down. In the Earth's orbit example used above, when you discover that in reality the orbit is not circular but in fact slightly elliptical, then using of a piece of string to represent gravity is no longer sufficient; a fixed length of string would allow only for a circular orbit. The analogy has broken down. With a bit of creative thinking from children or teachers, though, many analogies can be altered to become more accurate; a length of elastic would allow for an elliptical orbit. But all will break down in the end – if you connected any piece of string or elastic to the Sun it would just burn up!

Misconceptions

There is a risk, then, to using an analogy if it is not clear where it stops working. Misconceptions can be created about the new idea based on the characteristics of the analogy. For example, a commonly used analogy for explaining electricity draws a parallel with water flowing inside a pipe. This is useful to an extent and can partially explain how electricity moves in a wire. But it can reinforce, or even create, a common misconception that there should be a delay between connecting a light bulb to a battery and the bulb lighting up. People often consider the pipe to be empty until the battery 'fills it up with water' and the bulb will not light until the water has flowed around the circuit to reach it. In reality, there is no such delay – bulbs light instantaneously when connected correctly in a circuit, and it is not because the electricity is moving quickly (this can be tested with a really long wire). The problem here is that pipes can be full of water but they can also be empty. This is where the analogy breaks down: an electrical conductor is never empty of electrons, they are simply moving through the wire when electricity is flowing or stationary when disconnected. A better analogy for electricity, then, would be to show a cardboard tube full of tennis balls as a model of a wire.

Teaching Tip

Models and analogies are effective learning strategies

Robert Marzano's respected research into 4,000 teaching methods found that tasks that involve a learner identifying similarities and differences between two or more concepts was one of the most effective classroom strategies (Marzano, 1998).

This demonstrates that when the battery pushes a tennis ball (electron) into one end of the wire, all the electrons in the wire push one another along. The bulb lights up the instant it is connected to the battery as the wires are always full of electrons; the push from the battery just makes them flow.

Using creative approaches to make models and analogies more effective

So misconceptions can occur where models and analogies break down. To avoid this we can use strategies that explore their limitations. Ensure that children have the opportunity to be creative with the analogy, to test it in different scenarios, to question it, improve it and to say where they think it breaks down. It is crucial to spend time on discussion. Discussion challenges children's understanding by allowing them time to reflect on their own thinking, to explain their thinking to others, to question others and to answer questions. Children might even use thinking frames such as a double mind map to compare analogies to the concept they are representing (see Chapter 11, page 138).

We can ask learners to:

- analyse – What does this model explain well?
- criticize – What does it not show well? What is confusing?
- be creative – How can it be improved?
- create a user's guide to this model
- create and evaluate new models and analogies.

Assessment for learning

While the models by themselves might not give a clear picture of a child's understanding, the discussions around them are a great opportunity for assessment. Making notes on children's responses, or recording them to assess later, can reveal much about levels of understanding, misconceptions and confidence in the new ideas (Maloney and Curtis, 2012).

Teaching idea: Role playing electricity

Imagine a classroom with a large rectangle of masking tape on the carpet. The children are lined up in a queue around the rectangle, standing on the tape. In this scenario we are looking at a model of electricity flowing in a circuit. The analogy we are using is that the children moving along in a line are like the electricity flowing in a wire. One child is standing outside the rectangle, acting as the battery, giving each child a very gentle push as they pass. Another child, standing at the opposite side, is acting as a bulb. The rules have been discussed and the children know they can only move along the masking tape wire. So, after a pause in the role play for the removal of a short section of tape to leave a gap in the circuit, the children find that electricity can no longer flow despite the battery trying to push them around. The wire is full of children and when one cannot move forwards due to the gap the rest are halted too. There is simply nowhere to go.

So, how good is this model?

It shows well the basic concept that electricity is a flow of electrons within a conductor; it explains why a bulb lights up immediately and that electricity does not 'leak out' of unconnected wires, but the scale is far from correct, which leads to problems. The child acting as the bulb is raising their arms and lighting up every time a child goes past.

How can this model be improved?

The children are not happy that the bulb appears to be flashing:

Child A: The bulbs in our circuits don't flash.

Child B: Always keep one arm up but change arms when someone goes past.

Child C: But that looks like the bulb is flickering and they don't flicker . . . Hold both arms up while we are moving until we stop.

The children also suggest having a child as a switch, and discuss a suitable action:

Child B: The switch can just put their arm out to stop us moving.

Child A: But the switch makes a gap so they need to move the tape to make a gap.

Teacher: If you try to move the tape while the electricity is moving you might get your fingers hurt. How else could we show a gap?

The children decide the switch should hold out both arms with a gap between them and use the gap to block the movement.

Limitations: There are many, many more electrons moving along inside a wire in a circuit than there are children in the queue. The model does not explain why electricity cannot leave the wire – the children simply follow a notional rule.

There are many different ways this model can be improved, but this example shows how discussion can allow for creative suggestions that can be used to modify the model and allows the teacher to assess the children's understanding. Importantly, the children are challenging the model and looking to see where it agrees with real life and where it does not. The model itself is an engaging activity, but without the discussion around it there is little creativity involved and much less chance that the children will understand what they are doing.

Some examples of models and analogies by topic

Teaching idea: Plants – parts of a plant

Design and
Technology

Make model plants or model flowers. Encourage children to choose materials for the different parts depending on their functions and to explain their choices. For example, a straw may be used for the stem, illustrating that the stem transports water. Sticky tack may be used for the end of a stigma because it is sticky to catch the pollen.

Limitations: It can be difficult to find materials that represent both the functions and structure of the different parts. The inside of a stem is not hollow like a straw.

Teaching idea: Plants – pollination

Life Cycles

Make two giant paper flowers and ask the learners to use a giant bee or other flying insect to visit the flower, explaining how pollen is transferred. Can the children use this activity to create their own oral or written explanation of the process?

Limitations: Why do the insects visit? What's in it for them? Models used for this representation often fail to include the nectar that the insects come to collect. This is produced in nectaries usually found near the base of the carpel.

Teaching idea: Living things and their habitats – habitats and food chains

Arrange sticky notes on the classroom wall in groups each marked with the letter 'f'. These are shoals of fish. Ask six pupils to stand and explain that they are seals. Ask what they would feed on. Add some more seals, as food is plentiful. Ask the participants to 'freeze frame'. Once they have stopped, ask them to say what they are doing. Ask two other pupils to stand and announce that they are killer whales. Ask what killer whales eat. Explain that there is no running and that, when a killer whale touches a seal, it is 'eaten'.

Can the pupils now invent their own version? Can they develop the idea above to demonstrate a food web? There is further guidance on developing this model as a role play in Chapter 9 (page 120).

Limitations: The small populations used here allow species to become extinct very quickly. You could ask children to suggest what behaviour the seals could adopt to enable them to survive for longer.

Show the pupils a web-based population simulation such as Shodor's Rabbits and Wolves:

www.shodor.org/interactivate/activities/RabbitsAndWolves/ (tinyurl.com/bsf4au)

Teaching idea: Living things and their habitats – microorganisms

Glitter can be used to model how germs spread. During a lesson, ask two children to sprinkle glitter on their hands. They can then move around the classroom touching things and shaking hands with others. Before long, most other children will have some glitter on their hands too.

Limitations: This model shows only how germs can be transferred on contact. It does not show how many others are carried in the air.

Make models of bacteria and viruses from colourful magnified images. An internet image search for microorganisms reveals plenty of these images. Ask children to research the effects their microorganism can have.

Limitations: Many of these colourful images actually represent dull-coloured microbes. Colour is often added digitally.

PHSE

Teaching idea: Animals including humans – tooth decay

Use a 'tooth' the size of a sticky note, cut from thin polystyrene, and nail varnish remover or acetone (see Safety Tip). A couple of drops of acetone from a dropper on to the top of the tooth will begin to dissolve the polystyrene. A few more drops will begin to form a realistic-looking cavity. This could accompany the story of a pupil who did not look after their teeth. You could begin the story with the pupil eating sugary foods at breakfast. Challenge the pupils to continue the story as the demonstration progresses.

A safety sheet on using acetone can be found on the CLEAPSS website here:

> **Safety Tip**
>
> Acetone and most nail varnish removers are flammable and best handled by adults only. (The reaction is safe as it causes the expanded polystyrene to collapse, which releases air.)

www.cleapss.org.uk/attachments/article/0/SSS61.pdf?Secondary/Science/
Student%20Safety%20Sheets/ (tinyurl.com/qxvzpd3)

Limitations: The decay of the polystyrene is obviously much more rapid than decay in teeth. The acetone is a liquid, but sugar in solid form also causes tooth decay.

Teaching idea: Animals including humans – muscles

To simulate the action of a muscle, ask six pupils to join hands and stand in a line. Ask them to spread out and relax to show relaxed muscle (not pulling). Ask them to pull tightly together to show how the muscle tissue contracts and can pull things. Take it further by repeating this with one pupil at one end holding on to a solid wall or door handle (take care). This time as they contract it may be more obvious that if one end of the muscle is fixed then the pulling action will be at the other end. Ask them to say how this is like a real muscle and how it is different.

Limitations: Muscles can only contract to pull then relax. They cannot push. This is why they work in pairs. In this model the children could make the muscle push as well as pull.

Teaching idea: Animals including humans – the heart

Show pupils a liquid soap dispenser and discuss with them how it is like the heart. What other pumps can they think of, or systems that need them, e.g. central heating has a pump to push the warm water through the radiators, cars have a pump to get the fuel into the engine. A bicycle pump, for example, pushes air into a tyre.

Limitations: These simple pumps lack the complexity of the double-pumping action produced by the four chambers of the heart.

PHSE

Teaching idea: Animals including humans – the heart and lungs

See Chapter 9 (page 116) for a role-play activity that models the cardiovascular system. The heart pumps blood, carrying oxygen from the lungs to the body and blood carrying waste materials back to the lungs.

Teaching idea: States of matter – solids, liquids and gases

Using a play parachute and lightweight ball-pool balls, ask the pupils to move the parachute gently to make the balls vibrate slightly like particles of solids. Then shake the parachute slightly to make the balls move and flow around one another like particles of liquid. Finally, shake the parachute hard, forcing all the balls to fly in the air and fill the room like particles of gas. This works best in rooms with a reasonably low ceiling so the balls keep falling back on to the parachute. At each stage in the demonstration ask pupils to describe what they are observing and explain the phenomena. The amount of energy the children have to use represents the relative temperatures of the three states of matter.

A similar model uses a large clear box containing a small amount of rice or lentils to demonstrate how the particles in solids, liquids and gases move. As above, the amount of shaking represents the temperature.

Limitations: Although it can be done with careful control, the liquid state is relatively hard to achieve in these models. There is a tendency for the model to change quickly from the little movement required for the solid state to the much more vigorous bouncing around that represents a gas. Additionally, these models do not represent the forces between the particles that are present in real life.

See Chapter 9 (page 118) for role-play models of solids, liquids and gases where children act as particles.

Teaching idea: Rocks – types of rock

Geography

The differences between igneous, sedimentary and metamorphic rocks can be explored by making models of the three different types using grated chocolate. The grated chocolate represents rock sediment washed down rivers and into the sea. Three or four teaspoons of it can be sprinkled into a plastic bag inside a cup. Pressing down on the bag simulates the weight of further sediment, and enough pressing will cause the chocolate to stick together, forming a model of sedimentary rock. The model shares characteristics with real sedimentary rock in that it is weak and easily broken. If spoonsful of different-coloured chocolate are used, it also shows the layers often seen in these rocks.

Models of metamorphic rock can be made by placing some of the chocolate sedimentary rock into the bag and squeezing it into a ball using heat from the hands and greater force than before to represent the great temperatures and forces that turn sedimentary rocks into metamorphic rocks within the Earth's crust. This new model can be cut open to reveal a more densely packed structure that is stronger than before, illustrating typical characteristics of metamorphic rocks.

Igneous rocks are formed when molten rock solidifies. Therefore, to make a model the chocolate needs to be melted first. This can be done by heating chocolate in a disposable cup in hot water and then transferring the cup to a cool place once the chocolate has melted. The cup can be removed to show a chocolate igneous rock that is comparatively dense and strong. Children can discover the characteristics of the three types of rock by direct comparison and, if the rocks are prepared hygienically, what better way than by sampling each to feel the texture and strength of the rock as they bite!

Safety Tip

Due to the risks of using hot water with children it is recommended that igneous rocks are made as a teacher demonstration.

Safety Tip

Make sure the children have clean hands, and that all equipment is clean and hygienic.

Challenge children to create recipes for specific rocks such as granite. What can be added to represent the large grains? Fossils can also be modelled by adding small sterilized shells to the sedimentary process.

Can the children suggest which types of chocolate bar are most like the different rocks they learn about? The layers inside a Mars bar suggest a sedimentary rock, while anything with nuts or crispy pieces can represent conglomerate rocks, which contain many small pebbles cemented together.

Detailed instructions for making chocolate rocks can be found here:

www.jbprimaryscience.co.uk/rocks (tinyurl.com/lnedmz5)

Limitations: Chocolate rocks are much weaker than real rock and much quicker to make! The melting point of chocolate is much cooler than that of rock. Children may need to see a video of molten rock before they are happy to accept it can happen.

Thermal
Insulators

Teaching idea: Electricity – conductors and insulators

Ask children to work in groups to create role-play models for electrical conductors. Suggest that one child might act as the electricity trying to get through and the others as the conducting or insulating material. Can they think of an action for conductors that represents letting electricity pass through and one for insulators that shows the electricity trying but failing to get through?

Limitations: This model does not provide a good representation of the internal structure of conductors or insulators. Using a single child to represent the electricity suggests that electricity travels as a pulse rather than a continuous flow (see model below).

Teaching idea: Electricity – circuits

Using a rectangle of masking tape on the floor, children can act as electricity queuing up to move slowly round the circuit pushed by the battery. See earlier in this chapter for more information on how to structure this model.

A length of cardboard tube filled with tennis balls can be used as a model of electricity in a wire. This model shows why electricity flow is instantaneous. Pushing new particles into the tube causes all the balls to move.

Limitations: With this model it is rather easy for the tennis balls to roll out of the end of the tube. Electricity cannot flow out of the end of a wire unless there is a large enough push (voltage) to allow it to travel through the air.

Teaching idea: Light – how light travels

Light travels only in straight lines, but what else can only be straight? Spaghetti – uncooked of course! Ask children to create representations of how light reflects from mirrors or creates shadows, using spaghetti stuck to black card.

Use cardboard arrows to represent light travelling from a source then reflecting or scattering from an object. Ask children to create demonstrations to show how light travels in different situations.

Limitations: Light rays only ever represent part of the light coming from a source. We could draw a multitude of rays travelling in all the directions that light leaves the source.

Teaching idea: Forces – force arrows

Use cardboard arrows to represent forces. Ask a child to demonstrate the pushing of a chair or table, while others arrange the force arrows to reveal where the forces are acting. For example, arrows could show the pulling force and the frictional resistance of a chair being dragged across the floor. With older children, different-sized arrows could be used to show forces of different strengths.

Limitations: Children may assume that the arrow represents movement rather than a force. Make it clear that the arrows are like the pulling in a tug of war – a pull to the left will not result in movement to the left if there is an equal or larger pull to the right.

Teaching idea: Earth and space – night and day

Ask children to work in groups to create a role-play model that shows how different parts of the Earth have daylight at different times. The children might make an outward-facing circle and slowly rotate, changing their actions as they turn towards, and then away from, another child role playing the Sun. Ask the children to question this analogy and to explain where it breaks down.

Limitations: Here the Sun is portrayed as being smaller than the Earth and they are much too close together.

Teaching idea: Earth and space – the relative sizes and positions of the Earth, Sun and Moon

Using a football to represent the Sun, ask children to suggest suitable objects to be the Earth and the Moon. In fact, correctly scaled down, the Earth would be only 3 mm in diameter, and can be represented by a tiny piece of modelling clay or sticky tack on the end of a pencil. The Moon is even smaller and would be less than 1 mm in diameter in this model, so an even smaller piece of clay on the tip of a really sharp pencil will do. Ask children to suggest how far apart the Sun and Earth should be in this model, and ask the pupils holding the model to change position to show their suggestions. The children may be surprised to hear that this distance should be 30 metres, but they will be even more surprised to see that this model will not fit inside the classroom. It can be very effective if the child holding the Earth steps out of the classroom door and moves down the corridor to create the required gap, but it may be easier to relocate outside at this point. Once the positions of the Sun and Earth are established it will again be surprising to find that the Moon only needs to be 8 cm from the Earth.

With enough space, you could ask the children to begin to demonstrate the relevant orbits. This then leads in to the activity below.

The relative sizes and positions of the planets can be calculated for scale models at this website:

thinkzone.wlonk.com/SS/SolarSystemModel.php (tinyurl.com/8gpxjlc)

Find out more about building scale models of the solar system at this website:

http://www.exploratorium.edu/ronh/solar_system/ (tinyurl.com/22bug)

Limitations: The Earth's orbit is slightly elliptical; we have given average distances here. This model suggests a circular orbit.

Teaching idea: Earth and space – the orbits of the Earth and Moon

Challenge children to work in groups to act out the orbits of the Earth around the Sun and of the Moon around the Earth. There is more on how to do this in the playground in Chapter 10 (page 132).

Limitations: The Earth and Moon are much too large in relation to the Sun in this model, and much too close. Also the orbits will be acted out much too fast. You could suggest that the children work in slow motion to make the Earth take a year to orbit the Sun.

Teaching idea: Earth and space – the phases of the moon

This is a concept that both children and adults find confusing. This straightforward model allows us to understand it by seeing what is going on.

Set up a bright light source such as a mains spotlight or an overhead projector (warn the children not to look directly at the light source). Ask a child to sit on a stool or swivel chair in the beam of light and to hold up a white ball on a stick to represent the Moon (a ping-pong ball sticky-tacked to a pencil works well). The child's head represents the Earth. Ask the child to move the Moon so that it orbits their head, while watching carefully to observe the changes in the shadow on the Moon. All the phases, from a new moon to a full moon and back again, can be clearly seen.

See a video of this model on the BBC Stargazing LIVE website:

www.bbc.co.uk/programmes/p00n6zhl (tinyurl.com/ns9x2g6)

Limitations: Due to the relatively small distance between the Earth and Moon in this model eclipses happen far more often that in real life. A lunar eclipse is when the child moves the ball through the shadow of their head. A solar eclipse occurs when the ball is directly between the light source and the child's eyes. Encourage the child to hold the Moon higher than their head to see the Moon's phases without any eclipse.

Teaching idea: Computer simulations

There are many examples of computer simulations that are virtual models. Many of these are examples that could not be recreated in the real world.

There are links to many different simulations on the Kent ICT website. These include a parachute simulator, plant-growing simulations and even a design-a-satellite simulation:

www.kenttrustweb.org.uk/kentict/kentict_soft_simul.cfm (tinyurl.com/5tl94m4)

This link is to the original *Powers of Ten* simulation that allows you to zoom in from outer space to molecules and atoms:

www.powersof10.com (tinyurl.com/c32s3p)

There is a nice simulation of the human digestive system at this website:

http://kitses.com/animation/swfs/digestion.swf (tinyurl.com/2yfbzq)

Conclusion

With care, models and analogies will contribute to increased learning in class. By involving pupils in creating, describing and evaluating them you will maximize the children's understanding. Use of models and analogies can give children greater owner-ship over many key concepts. As learners gain confidence in creating them, they will learn to take more risks, to not fear being wrong and to be playful with ideas. As a tool for learning, the creation of models and analogies is a lifelong strategy that children can apply again and again to challenging situations. It enables us to think about our learning and about ourselves as learners.

Chapter summary

- Analogies are a creative way of thinking that reflects how the brain works.
- Models can be created that simulate scientific processes or objects.
- All models and analogies have limitations.
- Encourage children to challenge the limitations of models.
- Use discussion to explore these limitations.
- Give children responsibility for creating, changing and developing models.
- Encourage children to make their own analogies.

7

Images in science lessons

What will you learn from this chapter?

- A number of options for the use of images in science lessons.

- How to involve pupils.

- A range of exciting classroom examples.

Here we refer to the power of images for use in creative approaches in science teaching. Images have always been part of science, and in science teaching, sketches, diagrams, photographs and moving images all help to convey ideas. We live at a time when images are more easily available for teachers than has ever been the case. Fantastic images are only a few clicks away and are just as quickly shared with pupils on a range of screens we might use in class. This chapter links strongly with Chapter 4 because both make heavy use of ICT.

> **Teaching Tip**
>
> How easy is it for your class to access a camera?

The opportunity for learners to use images themselves has never been so good. Cameras of different kinds are more easily available now than they have ever been, they are simple to use and picture files can easily be used on computers, laptops and tablets.

Teaching idea: Images to inspire thought

When you are wanting to encourage creativity you might look for a hook for a topic or lesson introduction. Hooks can come in many forms: a visiting vet, a visit by the class to a museum, a film clip or video, still photographs, perhaps in a montage or sequence.

Growth

Figure 7.1 The world's tallest man?

Source: Science Kids website (http://www.thetallestman.com/robertpershingwadlow.htm)

For example, consider the photo of the world's tallest man in Figure 7.1. What does this picture say about human growth? What questions come to your mind? For example:

English

- Who is the man on the right?
- How tall is he?
- Why is he so tall?
- Is he normal and the other man very small?
- Did he keep on growing?
- Where did he buy his clothes?

- Did he live in a normal house?
- Was his diet normal?

Visual images are usually very meaningful to us. Who can fail to be inspired by moving images of things like volcanoes, plants and animals? There is a rich range of visual images available via the internet. Here are some examples to get you started:

http://video.nationalgeographic.co.uk/video/environment/environment-natural-disasters/volcanoes/volcanoes-101/

http://video.nationalgeographic.com/video/kids/green-kids/plants-kids/

http://animal.discovery.com/video-topics/pet-entertainment/funny-pet-videos/cute-baby-animals.htm

Large web-based resources store numerous videos on demand:

http://www.bbc.co.uk/learningzone/clips/topics/primary.shtml#science

Narrating a video clip

Could your class add a narration to a short clip (46 seconds) like this:

http://www.bbc.co.uk/learningzone/clips/images-of-the-earth-sun-and-moon/1589.html

First, they could create a simple storyboard around which to add their narration. Seconds are noted on the left in the list below.

06 rocket

08 Earth from orbit

11 the Moon

16 shadow of lunar lander

22 lunar buggy

26 Earth from the Moon

28 sunrise on Earth

34 the Sun

36 plants

40 clouds

Space

Here are the words of 10 and 11 year olds inspired by the film clip above:

- This US ship exploded out into space.

- This is a picture of Earth from the Moon, around is pitch-black darkness.

- Earth rise, on the Moon you can see the Earth come up.

- Half of the Earth is dark, asleep, half is light, awake!

- The Earth tilts in the direction of the Sun. It spins which creates day and night.

- This is the shadow of the lunar lander as it nears the Moon on its exciting voyage. This is the first shadow cast on the Moon's rocky surface by humans.

- Our special Earth, extraordinary and beautiful.

If learners struggle to fit their words in, simply pause the film while they discuss and write. Record their narration on computer, voice recorder or using audioboo.com.

English

However, sometimes the narration of these films is too advanced for young learners, so a further creative idea is to take a short clip and ask your learners to write and record a more appropriate narration. This can work well on MS PowerPoint, which has an option to add an audio narration.

Teaching idea: Still images

Photographs still offer a fantastic resource for teachers and learners – inspiring photographs, photographs that illustrate. Photographs taken by the learners provide a record of their work and make great illustrations for their recording of their work.

Alongside testing, children can record other aspects of their science. They can photograph aspects of the school, its site and the locality, e.g. materials we found in and around our school.

Forces

Another approach is to print out pictures related to science or pictures that children have taken, and ask the children to write and draw on the pictures to represent their thinking or ideas. In Figure 7.3, notes are made on a photograph of children studying forces with a tug of war.

Again websites provide teachers and learners with hundreds of science images, which can assist in lessons, project work and indeed almost any work in primary science. For example:

http://www.sciencekids.co.nz/images.html

Figure 7.2 A photograph taken by a pupil records part of a science investigation

A powerful image, such as the one of the bones in the lower arm – the radius and ulna in Figure 7.4 – can elicit a range of thoughts, ideas and questions. For example, learners could work in pairs and note what they see, as well as questions it inspires. Given a printed copy of this picture learners could add captions in the form of text to again note what they see, what they know and pose questions. This would be a useful assessment of what the learners currently know about bones and the skeleton.

Teaching idea: Video

Teachers now have a vast array of video material available for use in lessons. This material has the advantage that it shows things not otherwise available. What constitutes creative use of video? This is generally going to entail children being involved in the production of the video, but might also include:

*   learners narrating a short film
*   storyboarding a film and the production of a new episode
*   storyboarding a short film sequence

English

- script writing
- green screening.

Green screening (as mentioned in Chapter 4) allows children to create their own video sequences against any backdrop.

Figure 7.3 Photograph of tug of war with children's explanatory text

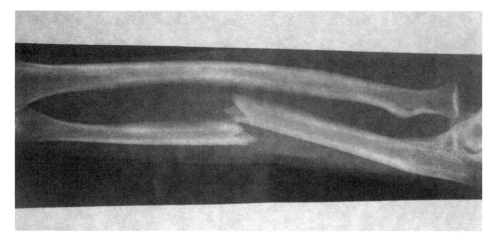

Figure 7.4 X-ray showing the radius and ulna in the human lower arm

Source: http://www.sciencekids.co.nz/images.html

Time-lapse video is particularly intriguing for young learners, especially when they have observed the same materials in real time themselves. Time-lapse video shows detail that is not revealed in normal observation. For example, there are several short clips available at:

http://www.haworth-village.org.uk/nature/time-lapse/thumbs.asp

Another example can be seen on the BBC website, where a shock wave caused by an explosion, which in real time moves too quickly to be seen, can be viewed slowed down:

http://www.bbc.co.uk/programmes/p006xzcl

Teaching idea: Children's videos and photos

Perhaps the strongest area for creativity is enabling learners to shoot film relevant to their science, recording aspects of their science to review or to present back to others. This can be video or a series of stills that record stages in the process of investigation.

At the initial stages of a lesson or investigation learners might go on a walk around the school site looking for examples, e.g. a sound safari. Their photographs of sound sources can be used in class to stimulate and organize their thoughts.

Teaching idea: Magnified images

Once difficult to access, magnified images are now commonplace. Many classrooms have visualizers that will magnify any materials and animals you have in class. Computer microscopes are now easy to use. All of this equipment is now much cheaper and more straightforward to use. Images are easy to enlarge, crop, adjust and embed in documents, etc. Websites such as:

http://legacy.mos.org/sln/SEM/flyfoot.html

Materials

also assist with magnified images. These reveal to children the world of the small and very small – detail that is beyond our eyes. This gives us the possibility of raising questions and inspiring a love of the world and a love of enquiry about the world.

The well-known *Powers of Ten* film shows both the very big and the very small, with stills from the film available on the *Powers of Ten* website:

http://www.powersof10.com

Some apps for tablet computers and smartphones can also zoom in on the very large and the very small. An example of an app that works in a similar way to the *Powers of Ten* video is available from Teaching Appz:

http://www.teachingappz.co.uk/listing/tick-baits-universe/

Various computer microscopes are available that allow the easy capture and use of magnified still and video images, which most children find intriguing.

Such resources for magnification can help to launch and contribute to science topics such as materials, animals, plants, and Earth in space.

Teaching idea: Animated pictures and posters

A number of web-based animated images have been developed for science teaching to illustrate principles, etc. Great care needs to be taken, though, as these cannot replace hands-on experience with real materials. Some animations are poor, lacking clarity and detail, and often a pause button! However, some deal with aspects of science that would be hard to illustrate in any other way. See, for example:

http://www.childrensuniversity.manchester.ac.uk/interactives/science/teeth andeating/buildamouth/

The best animations are invaluable, but how can we use them creatively? Can we hand them over to the children? Can they present them? Explain elements? Spot errors or shortcomings? Suggest improvements?

Teaching idea: Diagrams

Diagrams are the bread and butter of science books and materials. Can learners be put in the driving seat? Can they label, annotate and develop diagrams? Could they write a science textbook or booklet for younger pupils? Can they create one for themselves? Can they develop ways to use them as thinking tools?

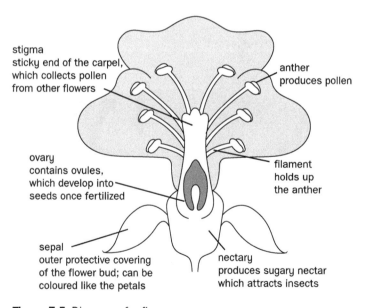

stigma
sticky end of the carpel, which collects pollen from other flowers

anther
produces pollen

ovary
contains ovules, which develop into seeds once fertilized

filament
holds up the anther

sepal
outer protective covering of the flower bud; can be coloured like the petals

nectary
produces sugary nectar which attracts insects

Figure 7.5 Diagram of a flower

Teaching idea: Graphic organizers

Ideas for using graphic organizers are also included in Chapter 11. Graphic organizers include diagrams, charts, graphs, flow charts, indeed any part-graphic representation of a phenomenon or system. Some learners find these visual resources very useful indeed; most learners find them useful. In science they offer a powerful set of resources for teachers to teach and learners to learn. Are we as teachers sometimes guilty of presenting these neatly finished and in a form that we expect to be simply digested? They are perhaps most useful when learners can engage with them, perhaps acting them out, explaining them to others, adapting and improving them.

Many websites offer graphic organizers, some of which have elements of interactivity, such as this one:

http://www.kscience.co.uk/animations/rock_cycle.htm

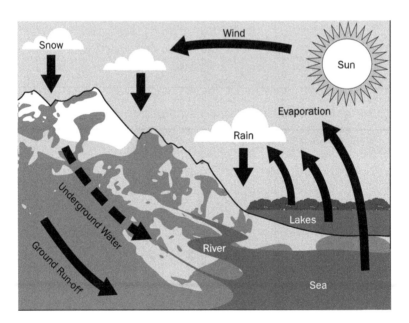

Figure 7.6 Graphic organizer of the water cycle

Teaching idea: Concept cartoons and concept maps

These widely used graphic organizers encourage interaction with science ideas. Concept maps (Novak and Gowin, 1984) ask the learner to establish a list of known concepts and then arrange this on a 'map' with interconnected lines and arrows. On the lines or arrows are added words by the learner, which articulate their understanding of the topic, as seen in Figure 7.7.

More terms can be added and relationships described. One advantage of this approach is that the resulting concept map is unique to the individual and very much belongs to them. It may contain errors and miss out important items, but it is personal representation of their understanding. This means that this is also a useful assessment tool.

Concept maps are usually created by individuals but can be constructed by pairs and groups.

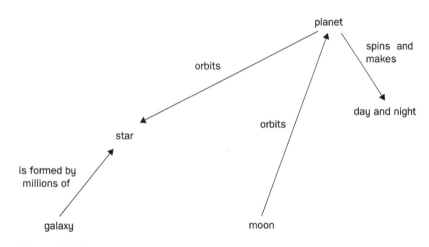

Figure 7.7 Concept map

English

Teaching idea: Concept cartoon

A concept cartoon (Figure 7.8) can be quickly sketched by yourself or your class but very often teachers begin with published examples such as the ones available from Stuart Naylor and Brenda Keogh in their book, *Concept Cartoons in Science Education* (2010), and on their websites, where several examples are available:

Materials

http://www.millgatehouse.co.uk/science/ccs (electrical circuits, friction and shadows)

http://www.conceptcartoons.com (thermal insulation)

Teaching idea: Augmented reality

Augmented reality allows tablet and other IT devices with cameras to reveal additional material linked to a text or picture. The tablet recognizes the picture or text and links to a website, which then reveals more text or images on-screen. In one example (Figure 7.9), a 3D image of Mars helps to bring to life a project to save a space colony on Mars in the year 2152. Further information about this project can be found at:

https://www.inspyro.co.uk/index.php/mars-project-summary-menu-link

Pupils can create similar links using QR codes (see Chapter 4), which can provide instant links to web-based materials.

English

Figure 7.8 Example of a concept cartoon

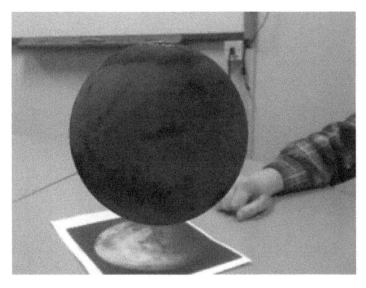

Figure 7.9 Example of augmented reality

Source: https://www.inspyro.co.uk

Teaching idea: ICT immersion environment

Since the advent of interactive whiteboards in the 1990s, we have become familiar with large projected images in classrooms. Some schools have classrooms with multiple projectors and some use has been made of so-called 'ICT immersion environments'. In these cases images are projected floor to ceiling on at least two walls, giving a sensation of being in the picture. A soundtrack often provides additional sensory stimulation. Thus learners can be surrounded by the sight and sound of a volcano, a rocket, an alien planet, a factory, a forest.

In one example, learners in the lesson listened to a recording from the American radio broadcast of *War of the Worlds* before listening to Holst's *Planets Suite* while they were surrounded by a giant image of an alien planet. After the lesson, one child commented: 'It gives you ideas, it's a lot better than sitting in class just listening to the teacher. It's not as good as in here with the sounds and the feelings that would happen in that particular place.'

Space

This strong sensory experience can inspire, excite and enthuse learners. They might explore every habitat on the planet, different cultures and time. They might be present when Alexander Graham Bell spoke for the first ever time on the telephone. He had had an accident and called his assistant for help. Could learners design their own immersion experience?

English

Figure 7.10 ICT immersion environment – an alien planet

Conclusion

Images have always offered a great deal to teachers and learners of science. They can convey a great deal of information in a form that, for many, is more accessible than the written word. Images can inspire and motivate; we can all remember images from space or the natural world that have filled us with awe and wonder. Things have changed now that images are very straightforward to access, create and manipulate, and learners can now use them as they might use any resource. As teachers we need to guide pupils who may inadvertently give too much emphasis to images and forget that the accompanying science, with associated explanations and discussions, is the more important.

Chapter summary

- A huge range of images is available for teachers.

- Image making has never been so straightforward.

- Images, image making and their use offer us and our learners a great opportunity for creativity in the science classroom.

8

Demonstrations

What will you learn from this chapter?

- Why use demonstrations?
- How demonstrations can support creative discussion.
- Creative approaches to demonstrations.
- Examples of creative demonstrations.

We are sure that many readers will be able to think of memorable science demonstrations they have learned from in the past. Yet, in a classroom where pupils are encouraged to learn by investigating, making decisions and even acting as real-life researchers (Kellet, 2005), asking them to observe a demonstration may appear to be a backward step. We want to show here that in all contexts demonstrations can be used to very good educational effect. In her review of research on the effective teaching of science, Wynne Harlen (1999) concluded:

> Providing first-hand experience . . . is often best served by a good demonstration or a field trip rather than 'hands on' practical work.

Most teachers will probably agree that the use of demonstrations in class should never restrict the children's experience of hands-on practical science but instead should provide an opportunity to be part of something that stimulates thought and discussion. As you read this chapter please ask yourself, is providing the demonstration all that is required?

In the opening chapter we discussed the idea of risk and risk taking for both teacher and pupil as a prerequisite for creativity. Demonstrations become creative when teachers push both the children and themselves to demonstrate, model and explain the science. While the demonstrations should be reliable and straightforward yet engaging, the way the teacher harnesses them may be less predictable in outcome.

Using demonstrations to stimulate creative discussion

Sawyer (2004) introduced the concept of teachers using disciplined improvisation within meaningful contexts. Whole-class discussion can be used as an example of this. The discipline comes from the teacher being clear about the boundaries within which the discussion can be allowed to explore freely, and from maintaining a focus on when it reaches those boundaries and needs to be refocused. The improvisation is in allowing the children to influence or control where the discussion ventures within those bounds. We would argue therefore that the element of improvisation encourages creativity by stimulating, and responding to, creative thinking by the children.

Demonstrations provide a thought-provoking focus for these improvised discussions and clearly signpost the centre of the territory that the discussion might explore. But, to embark on this journey, a teacher needs a certain confidence in their own subject knowledge and it may require you to allow the discussion to explore the limits of your own understanding. The latter is something that concerns some teachers, yet, as we have seen in Chapter 3, to establish what is known within a community and what then needs to be investigated is a very scientific way of working. In this situation children can be encouraged to record the unknowns as questions to be explored later.

To stimulate creative discussion, demonstrations may require the following:

- priming observers with what to look for
- repetition
- deconstruction, e.g. dividing into parts
- emphasis of scientific language
- descriptions by pupils of what did and did not happen
- questions from pupils about the demonstration
- further similar or less familiar examples.

One very creative and useful approach is to challenge pupils to explain which parts of a demonstration help them to understand the science and whether there are parts of the demonstration that are confusing.

Making demonstrations creative

This idea can, of course, be extended beyond simple discussions. Children's creative ideas might include changes to the demonstration to see the effects and predictions of what these effects may be. Challenge yourself, then, by aiming to shift responsibility to the children, encourage individuals or groups working together, to try the demonstration for themselves, to explore it, change it, to ask 'What if . . .?' This will reduce your control and introduce uncertainty for you as a teacher; however, it increases the potential for a positive educational effect.

Traditional demonstrations, where the teacher does everything and the children observe, can be used to stimulate creative discussion, as mentioned above. However, a more productive approach might be where some children are demonstrating and the teacher is evaluating their demonstration with the class; creativity can be seen in the suggestions and explanations the children provide. Or, taking it further, all the children are working in groups to prepare demonstrations for one another to observe and assess. They could even plan and make a film or podcast where they explain a phenomenon. We would suggest that, as a rule of thumb, teachers should constantly seek to shift responsibility and involvement in a demonstration to the pupils and include as many as possible.

> **Teaching Tip**
>
> **Responsibility**
> Give children responsibility for the demonstration.
> **Involvement**
> Involve as many children as possible.

Common misconceptions and mistakes can be highlighted by including, or asking children to include, deliberate mistakes in demonstrations. The children observing can then be asked to point these out and explain how to proceed correctly. For example, a demonstration of electrical conductors and insulators could involve showing a working circuit that includes a section of plastic. This will cause some confusion until the observers realize that the crocodile clips are attached to the plastic so close together that they are touching and the electricity is not flowing through the insulating plastic at all.

Ideas for creative demonstrations

Teaching idea: Animals including humans – body parts

Ask children to make labels or labelled drawings of external or internal parts of the body. Then ask them to attach them to a volunteer using masking tape.

Note: Be sensitive to children's feelings and avoid using the more private body parts in this demonstration. They should also be taught to ask permission before they touch.

Teaching idea: Plants – parts of a plant

Similar to above. Dress a child as a plant by adding paper leaves, shoots, roots and a flower. You could ask other children to attach these to the volunteer using masking tape.

Teaching idea: Plants – pollination

In spring or summer, ask children to pick two dandelion flowers complete with their stems. Show them how to rub the two flowers together to pollinate them, then put them in water and leave them in the classroom. Ask the children to predict what they think will happen. The flowers will close up and, after about a week, will look almost dead. However, after about two weeks they should open again to reveal a 'dandelion clock' seed head.

Dandelions are very useful flowers as the seeds can easily be collected by children and will germinate in only a few days in warm weather. The young plants will take some time to reach maturity and flower but, if you combine this with the demonstration above, you can easily show the whole life cycle of a flowering plant in just two or three weeks. In addition they are an obvious example of seed dispersal by wind.

Temperature

Teaching idea: States of matter – melting ice

English

Make a frozen ice hand by filling a rubber glove with water, folding over the end and using clips to seal it, then placing it in a freezer overnight. Children will be fascinated to watch the hand melt from solid to liquid. They will be keen to imagine where the hand may have come from, and this provides an excellent cross-curricular writing opportunity. Make the most of this by asking children to imagine being an ice creature, or snowman, who is melting, and to write a passage describing how this feels.

Large blocks of ice can be made by freezing ice cream containers or other plastic containers of water. These large blocks usually display interesting lines, bubbles and other features, and will take a surprisingly long time to melt.

Both of the above activities can be enhanced by adding food colouring to the water. As the water freezes, the colouring tends to move towards the centre of the ice block, creating a rather beautiful effect.

Teaching idea: States of matter – melting metal

Electricity

It can be helpful to demonstrate that materials other than ice and chocolate can melt. With great care, solder can be melted as a demonstration in class. Using an electric soldering iron over a heat-proof surface, solder melts very easily and forms pretty drips and splashes where it lands. This is best shown using a visualizer. The melted solder solidifies and cools very quickly and the newly solid solder splats can be safely handled by children.

Information is available online from CLEAPSS about the safe use of soldering irons:

Safety Tip

This should be done only as a teacher demonstration as a soldering iron gets very hot. Lead-free solder must be used. A risk assessment may be required.

www.ectinschools.org/pdfs/cleapss_rats_1.020.pdf (www.tinyurl.com/k7amdft)

Teaching idea: States of matter – evaporating and boiling water

Using a heat-proof glass saucepan or Pyrex beaker, heat water until it boils. Careful observation will reveal water evaporating as steam from the surface long before the water is boiling. Bubbles of steam can be seen forming at the bottom of the liquid, where it is warmest, before rising. The closest observation may reveal rippling convection currents in the liquid. Some of these effects may be seen even more clearly using a visualizer. Make sure pupils are kept well away from very hot water.

Safety Tip

Great care should be taken when using boiling water near pupils.

This demonstration could be extended by using a datalogger to record a line graph of the temperature of icy water as it increases to boiling point.

Teaching idea: States of matter – evaporation at room temperature

Evaporation can be demonstrated at room temperature. Wipe the top of a standard plastic-topped school table with a slightly damp cloth. Ask the pupils to describe what they observe as the damp patch evaporates. This demonstration works best with plain-coloured plastic table tops. It does not work well on wooden tops or fake wood grain as the evaporating liquid is hard to see.

This demonstration also works on a blackboard, but clean the board first to remove any leftover chalk dust. This allows the evaporation to be seen more clearly.

Teaching idea: Materials – condensation

It is not uncommon in hot weather for children to freeze water bottles at home overnight so they have cold water to drink at school. However, if a frozen bottle is left on the desk during the day, inevitably a puddle will form around the bottle. Children often come to the logical conclusion that the bottle is leaking. In fact, the water in the puddle forms when water vapour in the air comes into contact with the cold surface of the bottle and condenses on to it only to drip down on to the desk.

A nice demonstration on condensation, then, is to freeze clear plastic bottles three-quarters full of coloured water. Leave these on the tables and ask pupils to observe what happens. As time passes, water vapour from the air will condense on the outside of the bottles and then form a puddle. You can point out to the children that the bottles are not leaking as the water in the puddle is not coloured.

Very cold cans of fizzy drinks can also be used here, but there will be less condensation as the liquid inside is less cold. Canned drinks should not be frozen as the liquid expands as it freezes and the can will deform or split. Freezing liquid in plastic bottles is safe as they are more flexible, but make sure the bottle is not full so there is room for the freezing liquid to expand.

This demonstration is most effective in warm, humid or rainy weather. Much less condensation will appear on cold or dry days as there is less water vapour in the air in these conditions.

Teaching idea: States of matter – the water cycle

An open container of water sealed inside a clear plastic bag and left on a sunny windowsill will demonstrate some processes of the water cycle. Some water will evaporate from the container and condense in tiny droplets on the plastic bag. These droplets may become larger until they join up and run down to the bottom of the bag. This demonstration also works well using an inflated transparent balloon containing a little water. Stand the balloon on the windowsill and watch the water cycle repeat itself!

Teaching idea: States of matter – solids, liquids and gases – role play

See Chapter 9 for a role-play demonstration where children act out being particles of matter, behaving as those in a solid, a liquid and then a gas.

Teaching idea: States of matter – solids, liquids and gases – balloons

A simple demonstration of the different properties of the three states of matter involves presenting children with three similar-sized balloons, one full of air, one of water and one of ice. Children can discuss the differences such as the weight, the compressibility and whether they keep their shape.

Teaching idea: States of matter – air is not nothing

Push a clear cup upside down into a large clear tank of water to trap air inside the cup. The air cannot escape as the water is pushing it upwards into the cup. With care the air can be poured from the cup into a second cup that is also upside down but, this time, full of water. The air displaces water from the second cup. This is a nice reversal of an everyday process: the normal filling of an 'empty' cup with water. In this situation the cup is not really empty; it is full of air. When the water is poured in, the air is displaced and pushed out of the cup. This demonstration can be extended by sticking a £5 note inside the cup before putting it into the water. The element of risk that the money might get wet makes this very exciting.

There is a lovely video of upside-down divers using the effect here:

www.jbprimaryscience.co.uk/solids-liquids-and-gases (www.tinyurl.com/locx9ms)

Teaching idea: Properties and changes of materials – thermal conductivity

Water is a very good conductor of heat. This can be demonstrated by comparing the reaction of a balloon filled with water and a balloon filled with air when they are held over a candle, just above the flame. The air-filled balloon will burst, as you might expect, but the water-filled balloon does not. A balloon bursts when the rubber becomes hot and loses its strength. Because the water conducts the heat away from the balloon very effectively, the rubber does not get hot and the balloon does not burst.

Teaching idea: Properties and changes of materials – reversible changes

Drinks are made fizzy by dissolving carbon dioxide gas in the liquid under pressure. Dissolving is a reversible change and therefore the gas can be released from the liquid. This can be done by shaking or simply by leaving the drink open to the air, allowing the gas to precipitate back out of the liquid and diffuse away. But by far the most exciting method is to drop several Mentos sweets into a 2-litre bottle of Diet Coke. The texture of the surface of the sweets causes thousands of gas bubbles to occur, almost instantly resulting in a spectacular eruption of fizzy liquid from the bottle. The eruption can reach several metres high.

Teaching idea: Forces – making forces visible

Forces can be a tricky concept for children because we cannot see forces, we can only feel them. However, pulling forces can be made visible using elastic or rubber bands. The greater the force, the more the elastic will stretch. Similarly, pushing forces can be made visible using large sponges or lightly inflated balloons. In this case, the greater the pushing force, the more the shape of the balloon will deform.

Teaching idea: Forces – friction with hands

Friction between surfaces can be demonstrated by rubbing hands together. We can feel that there is some resisting force or grip, and that overcoming it creates heat. Children may link this to any burns they may have acquired in the past from trying to slide on carpet, or rope burns.

Teaching idea: Forces – friction with hairbrushes

The reasons for friction can be seen by rubbing the bristles of two hairbrushes together. The bristles interlock to an extent but can still push past one another. The greater the downward push on the upper brush, the harder it is to move it through the bristles of the lower brush. Pupils need to understand that even smooth-looking, smooth-feeling surfaces are in fact rough on a microscopic scale, and these rough surfaces tend to interlock like the bristles of hairbrushes.

Pupils could look at the following website, which shows magnified materials, revealing the roughness of a smooth surface. Zoom in on metal, down to atoms:

www.strangematterexhibit.com/index.html (tinyurl.com/cw2h9)

Teaching idea: Forces – lifting rice with friction

This is a slightly tricky demonstration to get the feel of, but children will enjoy having a go. Fill a straight-sided plastic container with rice then slide a pencil down the centre of the jar. Slide the pencil up and down several times, with a slight wiggle to shake the rice slightly so that the rice compacts down and closes up many of the air spaces. Top up the rice if necessary. With a bit of luck and patience, it is possible to lift the jar of rice by pulling up on the pencil.

Children could explore using different-shaped containers, replacing the pencil with a plastic spoon or other utensil, or investigating alternatives to rice in the jar. Could it work with lentils or sugar? How about dried peas?

Teaching idea: Forces – balanced and unbalanced forces

Ask some learners to conduct a tug of war under very careful supervision. Ask others to describe the forces on the rope, hands and feet, which result in the tug of war. As mentioned in Chapter 6, ask other children to arrange cardboard arrows to show the direction of the forces. Alternatively challenge two pupils to balance the forces in a tug of war: can they both pull with the same increasing force so that the rope never moves?

Teaching idea: Forces – why doesn't gravity pull us through the floor?

When standing stationary on the ground, the force of gravity must be balanced by an upward force otherwise we would begin to accelerate downwards! This force, known as a reaction, which balances gravity, can be illustrated by standing an object or pupil on a trampoline or exercise trampette. The springs stretch, but they are trying to pull back together and it is this pulling force that resists gravity.

Alternatively, measure the distance from the floor to the top of a standard metal-legged table then ask a pupil to sit on top in the middle and measure again. There will be a very slight bending of the table top. This bending creates an upward force that balances the pupil's weight.

Teaching idea: Forces – air resistance

The problem for pupils here is that both the force and the air are invisible. They will often think that air is nothing (see the states of matter demonstration, 'air is not nothing', above). Here are some ways by which pupils can feel or see the force of air resistance:

- comparing how fast flat and folded sheets of paper fall when dropped
- flapping large card sheets to move air in order to push newspaper fish along the floor
- making parachutes with tissue paper, thread and sticky tack
- running across the playground with and without a large sheet of cardboard
- making indoor kites using tissue paper, art straws and thin cotton thread.

In each case ask learners to say what they observe and why they think this happens.

Teaching idea: Forces – hovering balloons

This is another excellent demonstration of air resistance. Hold a hair-dryer so that it blows vertically upwards, then place a small semi-inflated balloon or ping-pong ball in the moving air. Gravity will pull the balloon down but the air resistance of the balloon due to the moving air will push the balloon up. These two forces balance, resulting in a balloon that hovers. There is actually a great deal more physics at work here, as the Bernoulli Effect keeps the floating balloon within the air stream.

Teaching idea: Electricity – static

There are many good demonstrations of static electricity, including rubbing a balloon on your hair and watching as the electrical attraction grips it to a wall.

A strip of clingfilm stuck to the edge of a table and hanging free will be attracted or repelled by a hand, depending on the charge (charge your hand by rubbing it in one direction on fabric).

Cutting shapes from thin craft foam and trying to stack them is entertaining as the pieces often repel so effectively that they jump off the stack.

Teaching idea: Light – reflections

In a darkened room, demonstrate light from different sources reflecting on shiny surfaces. Can the pupils describe exactly what they observe and how this changes with a matt surface? Can pupils demonstrate how a periscope works by reflecting the light from a torch from two or even three mirrors consecutively on to an object? Using a toy figure and making it 'famous' by putting it 'in the spotlight' is a nice context for this enquiry.

Teaching idea: Light – colour

On a sunny day, the fact that different-coloured objects scatter different-coloured light can be demonstrated by holding large sheets of coloured display backing paper in direct sunlight at the window and angling them so that much of the scattered light falls on the ceiling of the room. Careful observation and comparison of different colours will show that the light from the card actually changes the colour of a white ceiling slightly.

Teaching idea: Light – how the eye works

Some children will have heard that our eyes see things upside down. In fact, as light passes through the lens of the eye, it is inverted and forms a real upside-down image on the retina at the back of the eye. The retina contains light-sensitive nerve cells that send signals to the brain, which restores the image to the right way up. This effect can easily be demonstrated using a hand lens and white card. Dim the lights and ask children to hold a lens towards the window and to hold the card 20 centimetres or so behind. An inverted image will be seen on the card. The brighter the day, the clearer the image will be. The exact distance between the lens and card will depend on the shape of the lens, and the children will need to move the card until the image is clearly focused.

Teaching idea: Virtual experiments

Maths

Virtual experiments provide an interactive animation of a phenomenon or an investigation. Many teachers dislike such online demonstrations and prefer pupils to do the investigation themselves. This is a legitimate concern but virtual experiments can model or illustrate a learning outcome very effectively. They can provide instant, quantitative data, and so enable pupils to observe and to consider trends, patterns and anomalies in results more quickly. In this way they can be very useful in providing data for cross-curricular maths work.

These web-based demonstrations are safe and can suit a teacher as they can't go wrong, but equally they should be used cautiously. Teachers should adopt the features that assist, but avoid overuse. Be conscious that they can also rob pupils of valuable opportunities such as handling objects and equipment, dealing with difficulties, coping when things go wrong and seeing links to the real world.

For one example, go to BBC Science Clips website:

www.bbc.co.uk/schools/scienceclips/index_flash.shtml (tinyurl.com/3wcmn)

Teaching idea: Video demonstrations

Video allows pupils to see all sorts of phenomena filmed in the real world. It can remind them of things they have seen, extend the examples they have observed, and allows them to watch and then watch again. Short and carefully selected clips that illustrate scientific principles or science in the real world are often best for using in lessons. Bear in mind that many video clips intended for older pupils or adults can still be used with younger pupils. The images in many of these videos are often simpler and easier to learn from than the accompanying narration. Here it can be helpful to turn the sound off and provide your own age-appropriate commentary.

Here we suggest a number of links to helpful websites that provide useful short clips. There is also a list of video clip websites in Chapter 7 (page 85) that you can refer to.

The BBC's Class Clips website has a huge selection of excellent short clips for use in every subject:

www.bbc.co.uk/learningzone/clips (tinyurl.com/dj2fsb)

There are many good clips on the *Times Educational Supplement* resource-sharing website:

www.tes.co.uk/MyPublicProfile.aspx?uc=447531&event=21 (tinyurl.com/3awrwu7)

There are lots of useful YouTube clips on Jon Board's primary science website:

www.jbprimaryscience.co.uk (tinyurl.com/q5u9jvs)

Safety Tip

Take care when giving pupils access to online video. Make sure you follow the school's internet safety policy.

Teaching idea: Visualizers and digital microscopes

Technology to magnify materials and actions allows a form of demonstration not previously possible. This equipment allows a whole class to observe the movement of a snail or close-up detail of the burning of a rubber band. Pupils can observe and discuss together what they see. Digital microscopes reveal fascinating detail of the structure of mini-beasts, plant material or human skin. (See more about this in Chapter 4 on ICT, page 47.)

Chapter summary

Key learning points on using demonstrations:

- you cannot over-emphasize scientific language
- do be prepared to improvise
- ask pupils to film demonstrations and provide a commentary
- ask pupils to discuss demonstrations
- ask pupils to create a podcast to explain demonstrations
- ask pupils to write a science explanation
- put the pupils in charge
- if things go wrong, use this opportunity to explore, repeat and explain.

9
Dance and drama

What will you learn from this chapter?
- When you might use dance and drama.
- The potential for dance and drama in science teaching.
- The value of dance and drama for developing literacy.

We hope that we have established that science is a creative subject and that science education should reflect this. Primary teachers tend to know something of the value of practical demonstrations and hands-on science. Many will have used movement in lessons and will have experienced how dance and drama can make science accessible to all learners.

Teaching idea: Particles dance

Perhaps the best-known dance in science is the particles dance, where learners move their bodies so as to replicate in some way the movement of particles – the solid, then liquid and gaseous states of water.

A group of learners begin with arms interlocked, close together with only slight vibrating, the only movement. The teacher might then use a tambour or tambourine to signal that, slowly, heat energy is being added. The learners vibrate a little more and the interlocked arms prepare to release to simulate melting. With more 'heat' from the teacher and the signal 'melt', the children release arms and, still close together, can move slowly in relation to one another. With more heat applied, they can begin to move more vigorously, but still close together. As heat is added, movement is increased and boiling is simulated. The signal 'evaporation increases' means that individual children

Materials

move quickly yet safely away from the group as they are now representing water vapour, the gaseous form of water.

Dance and drama are by their nature creative. Learners will make suggestions for a dance when in a more formal lesson they might be reluctant to make a suggestion. Creative movement, as you know, is best stimulated by the observation of movement, e.g. observing an earthworm move, or by a sound, e.g. music or a drum beat for the 'lub, dub' of the heartbeat.

Lessons like this with a strong movement element allow all learners to participate. This can be ideal for learners who have difficulty with language as they can express ideas with their bodies. Opportunity to then talk about the dance or drama can provide excellent scaffolding for learning.

You will get the most out of dance and drama in science if you enable discussion about the movement and the science. Can learners say what they are representing at this point in the role play? Can they say what is happening? Why this is important? What will happen next? Audio and video recordings can add considerable value to these activities. Lessons with these elements are often very memorable (Cross and Bowden, 2009) and as such aid pupils' learning of science.

The dividing line between role play, drama and dance is difficult to draw and, we would suggest, not meaningful for our purposes here. What is important is the expression, opportunity to feel the movement, and the stimulus to think and rethink about a phenomenon or idea. Movement of our bodies gives us another way to consider an idea and, for many of us, a very powerful way to reflect on what we see around us. Such approaches are inherently inclusive because they don't rely heavily on previous knowledge.

> **Safety Tip**
>
> Make sure learners have sufficient space to avoid collisions with one another and furniture.

Dance

Dance and movement are almost universally loved by young children, who love to move to music. Getting them to listen to the speed and quality of a beating drum usually initiates spontaneous movement. Dances can occur linked to many parts of science. Ask the learners to observe snails and slugs prior to moving like a slug or snail. Can the learners find words to describe the movement they observe? Can they suggest why the animal moves in this way? After moving to a larger space, can they now develop a dance that will show the movement of a snail from withdrawn in its shell to moving and searching for food?

Teaching idea: Burning dance

Talk to learners about heat and light, and the fact that many humans still get their heat and light from flames and fire. You might explain that the fuel is a store of chemical energy from, say, a tree that once got its energy from the Sun.

Taking appropriate safety precautions (supervision and a handy bucket of sand or water) allows learners to observe a match or candle burning. Ask them in groups to describe the colour, the movement, any smell. Then ask them to make a shape to show the match before it is ignited. After a verbal signal, ask them to show how they ignite and slowly begin to burn. Can they make the shape of the flames with their body and arms? Can they move their body in the way that the flames move?

Energy

Practise different stages of ignition, burning and then being blown out (take care with hot wax if using candles). Expect the learners to observe the stages carefully. For example, as a match burns it curls up.

Can they bring the various parts of the dance together in one longer dance? Can they dance this alone but then in pairs? Can they talk about the stages? About what is happening?

Teaching idea: Gear wheels dance

You can reinforce how gear wheels mesh and turn in different directions by asking learners to observe and then copy, using the head, elbows, hips and knees as the cog teeth on individual gear wheels. This lesson works best with a set of large gear wheels or smaller cog wheels on a visualizer, which can be turned to demonstrate the change of direction and change of speed. Learners can then work in pairs to demonstrate how one gear wheel is the driver and the other is the driven gear.

Mechanisms

You can demonstrate that, if the two gear wheels are the same size with the same number of teeth or cogs, they will rotate at the same speed. If, however, one is smaller with fewer teeth, the smaller one will have to rotate faster. Thus the learners can develop another dance to show this.

Design and Technology

This is easily extended to a gear train where several gear wheels mesh in a line so the drive gear rotates them all. Thus several children can dance together.

Useful pictures and animations can help support you here too:

http://www.youtube.com/watch?v=D_i3PJIYtuY (wheels and gears)

http://bowlesphysics.com/images/Robotics_-_Gears_and_Gear_Ratios.pdf (types of gears)

These dances can become complex and exciting, as when schools have visited a science museum and linked the dance to working machines.

Teaching idea: The 'life of a leaf' dance

Plants

The importance of plants and their leaves can be reinforced strongly when, after observing a number of plants and seedlings, learners create a dance about leaves. This dance might be in several sections: germination and growth, the rolling out of a leaf, leaf growth, photosynthesis, leaf wilting and leaf fall.

Teaching idea: Life cycles dances

The life cycles of a number of animals lend themselves to a dance. These include:

Living Things

- frog
- butterfly
- a mammal, e.g. a lion
- a bird
- a fish, e.g. an eel
- invertebrates, e.g. a snail.

One class were asked to observe the eggs of cabbage white butterflies, which over a series of days hatched to reveal caterpillars. They were able to watch film of an emerging caterpillar. The learners were asked to roll up in a ball as if inside the egg and then eat their way out of the egg before climbing out and moving on to leaves, which then became the next meal. Their written descriptions later that day were highly animated.

Video of the phenomenon can assist in stimulating movement and thought. For example:

http://www.haworth-village.org.uk/nature/time-lapse/time-lapse.asp?pic=7

Role play

Role play is similar to dance but is perhaps more overtly aimed at representing and explaining science ideas. Like dance it quickly becomes creative when learners add to or adapt the dance.

Teaching idea: Electricity – how electricity flows

Use masking tape to mark out a large rectangle on the floor to be the wires of a circuit. Choose three pupils to act as a battery, a switch and a bulb, then ask all the others to stand on the wires in a queue so that they are ready to follow each other around the circuit. The circuit should be small enough that the pupils are standing close to one another all the way around. Explain to the pupils that they are particles that are in the wires (electrons) and that these can move when given a push by the battery. We call this movement of electrons electricity. Ask the pupil representing the battery to stand next to the wire giving the electrons a gentle push as they go past. This is where energy in the battery is used to push electrons. Ask this pupil to say 'push' each time so all the 'electrons' can hear. This reinforces the idea that the battery provides a push to the electrons. Ask the pupil representing the bulb to stand next to the wire and to raise their arms when the electrons are moving and lower them if they stop. Ask the pupil representing the switch to stand next to the wire and to hold their arms out in front of them but with a gap between them. When the switch is off, the pupil steps forward

Figure 9.1 Learners model the flow of electricity around a circuit

Electricity

Design and Technology

blocking the movement of the electrons with their 'gap'. When the switch is on, the pupil steps back so there is no gap in the circuit.

Teaching idea: Electricity – resistance

Energy

Arrange approximately 12 pupils, in pairs, queuing. Explain that they are particles in a wire made of conductive material. Ask them to assist a pupil who is an electron (perhaps holding a ball or a balloon) as this pupil moves between the two lines. Repeat this, modelling a more resistant material and with a totally resistant material.

PSHE

Teaching idea: Animal biology – the heart and lungs

Energy

After arranging a figure of eight on the floor with chalk or masking tape, add labels for the heart, lungs and body. Ask pupils to walk around the figure of eight as if they were red blood cells. As they enter one side of the heart they are pumped towards the lungs; on returning to the heart they are pumped towards the body. Ask them periodically to say where they are and where they are going next. At the lungs they can collect inflated balloons representing oxygen. These can be carried to the body, where the oxygen is used, shown by bursting the balloons. The carbon dioxide waste produced by the body (the burst balloon) is carried back, via the heart, to the lungs, where it is removed from the blood. Having experienced the red blood cells' journey around the body in this practical way, ask the pupils to describe it. This shows how gases, waste and food energy are transported around the body.

Common misconception

'The heart has just one chamber giving just one push'

Try this as a whole-class demonstration in the hall or on the playground.

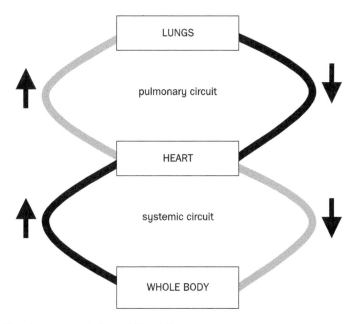

Figure 9.2 Simple representation of blood flow

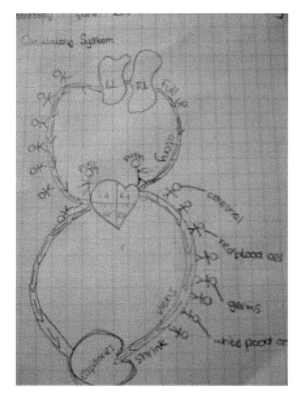

Figure 9.3 Pupil plan of a model of the circulatory system

Figure 9.4 In a science lesson, pupils chalk out their giant model of the circulatory system

Teaching idea: Solid, liquid and gas particles

Materials

Ask pupils to act as particles of a solid, with hands on one another's shoulders to represent bonds. They should be vibrating but not moving. Heating the solid means giving it more energy so the vibrations get larger until hands slip off shoulders and the bonds break. Now the particles can walk around at the front of the classroom – the solid has melted into a liquid. The faster-moving particles can evaporate at the 'surface' and move a bit more quickly around the room – no running. The particles remaining in the liquid can be given more energy by heating – children may suggest that pupil observers or the teacher heat the liquid by waving their outstretched arms towards it, miming a flame. The heat makes the particles in the liquid move slightly faster until the liquid boils to create a gas with all the particles moving around the room. This could be extended to create a cross-curricular dance. Can pupils suggest different movements for the particles? Can they think of other ways to improve the model?

Common misconception

'In very cold solids, particles are still'

Teaching idea: Sound waves

Music

With pupils standing in a line holding hands they can pass on a hand squeeze or make a Mexican wave to demonstrate the way a wave travels. This can be extended by standing the pupils in concentric circles with the Mexican wave starting from the middle and spreading out in all directions to show how sound travels.

One alternative is to have pupils standing as if in a queue, a few centimetres apart. Warn them that you are going to give a gentle push and they must not fall. Give the last pupil in the queue a small, gentle push on the back. Here pupils see how the sound energy travels from particle to particle.

Energy

Another way is to have a line of five to eight pupils standing closely side by side pretending to be air particles. A pupil can shout a word at one end of the line, another can listen at the other end. When the sound starts, each pupil in the line starts to vibrate in turn because the pupil next to them is wobbling into them. This continues until the last air particle is vibrating and the listening pupil can 'hear' the sound. It's fun to repeat this in slow motion.

Pupils should have seen the waves caused when an object is dropped in water. Ask a pupil to demonstrate this and the others to explain why this is like sound waves.

There is a very useful video here:

> https://www.youtube.com/watch?v=Yi3LW5riHfc

Teaching idea: Pollination and fertilization

Life
Processes

These are two terms that are often confused in a process that is often misunderstood. How could learners represent these ideas in dance? You might explain that the flower is like a machine for making seeds, but it requires pollen to make the seed complete.

One way it has been represented is by one child standing centrally as the stigma – their head represents the sticky top of the stigma awaiting pollen and their feet are the nectary making sugary nectar. Five or six others standing around them facing the stigma represent stamen. On the head of each stamen is pollen (you could scatter confetti or similar paper on their heads). Around these children is another circle of children who are the colourful petals.

Common misconception

'Petals are there to make the flower pretty for us'

Now a child is selected to represent the flying insect, the bee. He or she is attracted by the petals, which are a signal that, within, nectar will be found. This is the food for the insect. The 'bee' now has to push past the leaves and importantly the stamen, picking up pollen on their body. As they climb past the stigma some pollen is deposited on the stigma (this represents self-pollination).

Explain that, after the bee has collected nectar, it has to go past the stigma and stamen again, dropping and picking up more pollen. The system works best when the bee visits many flowers of the same type, and transports pollen from one plant to other plants of the same kind. The bees end up covered in pollen.

As with other role play and dances, repeat it with learners giving a commentary and later filming it or describing it.

Teaching idea: Habitats/food chains

Energy

Prior to a lesson prepare 50 sticky notes with a letter 'i' on them and stick them all around the walls and furniture of the room. As children enter the room they will be interested to know what these are for. At the right point in the lesson, explain that these are insects, perhaps greenfly, and that six children are invited to be birds and 'fly' around the room collecting or 'eating' the insects. Check that they understand where the insects get their food from and that this energy has come from the Sun. Allow them to start and ask what would happen to the size of population of the insects and the population of birds. Ask another two to be birds, to represent the increasing bird population. Can the learners track the energy from the Sun to plants to insects to the birds? Now introduce two children as hawks. What do these eat? Small mammals and birds! Without running, ask them to *walk* around the room to touch on the shoulder the 'birds'. The birds must agree not to run. Can the learners explain the terms predator? Prey? Can they explain how the dance drama illustrates a food chain like this? Make sure that they draw the arrows in the right direction, showing the direction in which the energy goes.

Common misconception

'In a food chain the arrow shows who eats whom'

Figure 9.5 A food chain

There is a predator/prey simulation online at:

http://www.shodor.org/interactivate/activities/RabbitsAndWolves/

Teaching idea: Solar system

A classic primary role play would see you in the school hall with perhaps the curtains closed and a child holding a torch standing centrally as the Sun. At a radius of a metre you might mark the circumference of a circle around that child and on this line a child stands holding a marble-sized piece of plasticine.

See the model of the solar system to scale in Chapter 6 (page 80).

Space

Teaching idea: Freeze-frame tableaux

Freeze-frame tableaux provide a very straightforward way in which learners can represent an idea, and offer an excellent medium for cross-curricular learning. While they could be used to represent inanimate objects like the gear wheels in a race or the planets, these often work best when depicting people or events, e.g. people harvesting food, people in a hospital. In these cases the group have to talk about the context and what would be happening in the setting. Once they are clear about this they can spend some time planning poses and how they will arrange the tableaux.

Darwin

A further option is to represent part of the life of a famous scientist or inventor, e.g. Alexander Graham Bell making the first ever phone call just as he spilt acid on himself, thus crying for help down the phone.

The example in Figure 9.6 shows Year 6 pupils creating a science tableau of Charles Darwin noting the shape of the shells of the giant tortoise as Captain Fitzroy berates him for his ideas about evolution. This example is further developed in Chapter 7, when it is used as a basis for further discussion.

Teaching idea: Green screening

Green screens allow learners to act or role play in front of any setting. They can become journalists reporting on a discovery, explorers describing a new habitat, astronauts talking about a visit to a planet. Of course, a very similar effect can be achieved with a straightforward digital recording where learners describe a setting and some science relating to it (see Chapter 4).

Figure 9.6 Year 6 pupils create a science tableau depicting Charles Darwin

Conclusion

Dance and drama can change an otherwise quite dry, closed lesson into something more exciting and expansive. Children usually recognize immediately that in this context there is opportunity for expression, for trying out ideas, for playfulness. If the children don't yet see science as creative then they should see dance and drama as creative. Science can then benefit from this as enthusiasm and creativity can be infectious. These are great opportunities for learners to explore ideas and the language around them – this is perhaps the role of the teacher, so establish a context that is open and risk friendly, and ensure that science ideas, language and skills remain at the forefront. This should be obvious when you note that your lesson objectives are still science based (they might even use the term creative), but your vehicle for teaching it enables creative thought and action.

Chapter summary

- Dance is a wonderful medium in which to be creative.
- Many science principles can be explored through dance.
- Dance allows us to develop science vocabulary in a meaningful context.

10

Playground science

What will you learn from this chapter?

- How playground science works.
- How playground science encourages creativity and leads to effective collaborative learning.
- Some examples of playground science activities.

If you have ever taken a class of children into a playground you will know that it changes things. It changes how the children behave, it changes how you communicate with them and it changes their expectations of the lesson. Going outside releases children from the organizational structure of the classroom. This change in structure provides the opportunity to feel less constrained; an opportunity for the children to have the freedom to be more creative.

This chapter is not about outdoor nature study. The activities discussed here use diagrams, sketches and words drawn on the playground with chalk to assist with role play, games and discussion; a chalk stage on which to act out a role play, a chalk board on which to play a game. The words and diagrams are used in lessons and then left for children to play with during the day.

The diagrams should be large and clear, but they are not always neat. It is not easy to draw perfectly straight lines with chalk and not usually necessary. What is important is the discussion that happens as part of the activity; discussion about the science, the concepts and the associated vocabulary.

In playground science, children can collaborate in groups to modify, improve and control the way the activities work. Because of this, they feel an ownership of the activity and a sense of wanting to share it with others. Older children have been observed teaching younger ones, younger teaching older and classmates playing together. Peer-to-peer learning is an implicit part of playground science.

During playtime, the combination of chalk reminders left on the playground and the children's sense of ownership promotes free play based around the science activities. The independence the children feel at playtime means they tend to be very creative in modifying and reorganizing the activities to suit their particular group of friends, and children can often be seen teaching the activity to those in different classes or even different year groups.

Children's thoughts on playground science

L: It's a good way to remember because you're interacting.

M: If you just watched it, you think it makes sense. But when you come to do it you're like, OK, how does that work and you do it and you understand.

Z: If it's boring, children don't want to listen but you made it into a fun way and when you speak children want to listen more because they think it's going to be more fun. Because you're like . . . just turning around but you're learning at the same time.

Playground science has a great deal to offer in terms of creative development. Drawing on the playground, an environment designed for playful behaviour, children seem comfortable playing with ideas. Creating actions and role play fire the imagination, and the less familiar format of the lessons appears to promote original thinking. The peer-to-peer aspect of reviewing work, teaching games and sharing ideas encourages children to assess the value of what they have created.

Collaborative learning and playground science

The educational benefits of collaborative learning are well established (Howe and Mercer, 2007) and a review of research into group work by Galton and Hargreaves (2007) concluded that it not only improves the quality of children's discussions about the topic, but also improves both their social relationships and their relationship with the teacher. However, despite its effectiveness, this kind of group work has been found to be used only infrequently within core subjects (Kutnick *et al.*, 2007).

Playground science is a great opportunity for effective group work. A key principle is that the children are encouraged to talk to one another about what they are drawing, or their part in the game or role play. They have to explain their understanding of the science to others in order to complete the activities. This reflects Vygotsky's ideas of social constructivism – that people achieve greater attainment when working in groups as the dialogue and interaction cause them to consider and challenge their own understanding (Vygotsky, 1986).

Encouraging children to be guides as part of the lesson, showing others how to use the activities they have developed, not only increases the likelihood of participation later on in the day, but also creates another opportunity for this social sharing of ideas. However, the right atmosphere needs to be established. The skills required for effective collaborative learning should to be modelled, encouraged and rewarded at all times. Children need to learn to listen to one another, and need thinking time to decide whether they agree or disagree, or whether they are not sure. As teachers we should encourage children to question one another's thinking and to ask for more detail when they do not understand the ideas being explained by others. Being 'not sure' is an important option, and asking why someone is 'not sure' is often more revealing than asking those who are. This is perhaps a good opportunity to teach some of the language of scientific discourse, e.g. 'Can I/we just check that?', 'Are we sure about that?', 'Have we/I got that right?', 'I need to get that clear in my mind', 'Can you show me how that works?', 'Can you explain that again?' Put these phrases up on the classroom wall and model them.

Teachers can make this easier for children by considering the make-up of each group carefully. Personalities and friendships need to be considered, but so too does group size. Working in a group of six is much more complex than a group of three or four. A trio contains only three different possibilities for one-to-one communication: A–B, A–C and B–C. A group of four presents six possibilities, but a group of six allows for 15 different combinations, with the number of possible interactions growing far faster than the number of pupils in the group. Working in groups of three or four therefore appears to be the optimum for constructive collaboration since paired work can constrain discussion (McGregor, cited in Oversby, 2012).

Teachers are sometimes reluctant to work outdoors, expressing concerns about children's behaviour (Boyd, 2013). However, when children are presented with well-planned group activities that involve decision-making tasks, the chance of disruption due to behavioural concerns is actually reduced (Baines *et al.*, 2009).

A creative playground science lesson

For an example of playground science let us consider a lower Key Stage 2 lesson with the objective of linking food chains to habitats. The lesson could begin in the classroom with a discussion on what the children already know about food chains, and exploring the vocabulary of producer, consumer, predator and prey. There is a discussion to be had about expectations of behaviour in the playground, and about hygiene and safety, with children suggesting how they can prevent the spread of germs from the playground surface. Working in small groups of three or four, the first task in the playground is for each group to choose a habitat – rainforest, arctic, pond, etc. – and to use chalk to draw and label their chosen habitat and the organisms within it. Some groups might be using reference material for support.

The whole class could be gathered around one area to hear a description of the habitat by the group, and could suggest additions or corrections the group could make: 'You need to add some plants', 'Lions don't live in the rainforest.' Having modelled this process, groups can now take turns visiting other groups to repeat this peer assessment procedure. This part of the process helps children to see the value of what they are creating.

The next step involves imagination and originality. In this case, the children could draw arrows to demonstrate food chains within their habitat and then create a sequence of actions that shows the food chains being acted out. In this situation it is only a small

Figure 10.1 Creating a habitat

logical step for the children to develop the idea of a food chain into a food web showing the more complex interrelated feeding patterns within a habitat.

With enough time, the children could again visit other groups for a presentation involving the role-play demonstration of the food chain or food web. Here again there is an opportunity for self- and peer assessment, as well as scientific dialogue: 'We didn't know what other plants to draw', 'Birds eat spiders as well as caterpillars. You could add spiders in there.'

Photographs or video can be taken by the teacher and used back in class to recap on the key learning points from the lesson. Children can be asked to say what they have learned from their own work or from that of others.

This kind of activity takes time but many would see such an inclusive option as time well spent. Children outside the classroom tend to relax and be very willing to explore, both physically and through talk, ideas they have or ones they come across. The increased freedom ties in with ideas of the social aspects of learning – that people learn much of what they do in social settings. They test their ideas and those of others in the social context. With known classmates they feel safe to express an idea before sharing it with an adult. Contexts such as this can have a positive effect on the autonomy of the learner (Boud, 1987).

Teaching Tip

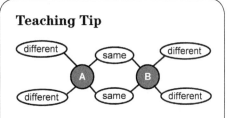

Figure 10.2

Use graphic organizers to create playground science activities. Children could develop role play to show cause and effect or how something changes with time. See Chapter 11 (page 138).

More examples of playground science activities

Teaching idea: Plants – parts of a plant

Children can draw a giant plant then develop a role play that illustrates the function of the different parts. This could involve acting as water to show it being absorbed from the soil into the roots then transported by the stem to the leaves. Or the focus might be the function of the flower in being pollinated by insects then growing into a seed-producing fruit.

With older children, this activity could be used as an exploration of photosynthesis. Children could act as water, carbon dioxide and sunlight coming to the leaves and being photosynthesized into food for the plant and waste oxygen given out by the leaves.

Teaching idea: Plants – parts of a flower

Similar to the previous activity, but this time children draw and label the detail of the structure of the flower then act out the transfer of pollen from the stamens of one flower to the stigma of another. The growth of a pollen tube inside the carpel, fertilization and the growth of the seed could all be included here. Some children could act as insects, transferring pollen from group to group. Bean bags or other PE equipment could be used to represent pollen.

Teaching idea: Animals, including humans – the heart and lungs

See Chapter 9 (page 116) for an introduction to this role-play activity where there are many different parts for children to play. They can act as the blood moving around the circulatory system or as the heart pumping the blood, the lungs adding oxygen and removing carbon dioxide, or as the body taking the oxygen it needs from the blood and producing the carbon dioxide. In the playground the veins, arteries, heart, lungs and body can all be drawn with chalk

Teaching idea: Animals, including humans – the digestive system

A similar activity to the heart and lungs one, above, where the children draw a simplified digestive system and then take on the role of food passing through the system being digested, or of the active parts of the system such as the teeth, the acid in the stomach or the villi in the intestine removing water from the waste.

Teaching idea: Living things in their habitats – food chains and food webs

See the example given earlier in this chapter (page 125).

Ask children to think of an animal and its food; they should either draw the animal or write its name and then, beside it, its food. They can then draw an arrow from the food to the animal. Useful discussion here would be about the energy in the food

Figure 10.3 At playtime, children continue to play on the giant circulatory system

transferring to the animal, and terms such as consume, food, carnivore, herbivore, predator and prey. The drawing can be added to if another animal is identified that preys on the first animal.

seeds $\longrightarrow$ mouse $\longrightarrow$ owl

On the playground children can act out the roles of the animals in the food chain. Useful discussion can occur, with children talking about what might happen in years when there is an abundance of seeds and in years when bad weather reduces the number of seeds.

This idea of representing food chains can be developed into a food web, with more interconnectedness.

Teaching idea: Living things in their habitats – life cycles

Children can be asked to sketch out the stages in a life cycle using drawings, words and arrows. They can then walk around the cycle describing the stages to others and developing actions to represent each stage.

Teaching idea: Everyday materials – materials game

This is a simple game that could start by simply asking the children to run to and touch an object made of a specific material. It could be followed up by asking children to use chalk arrows to label materials or to link objects made of certain materials to a giant text box with information about that material.

Teaching idea: States of matter – solids, liquids and gases

This is an adaptation of the particles dance from Chapter 9 (page 111). There are many ways this could be represented diagrammatically but, as an example, the children could create a huge diagram with three different sections, one each for solid, liquid and gas. The gas section could be larger to show they understand that gases expand to fill the space, and the different sections could be connected with arrows labelled with the relevant names of the changes of state required. The children can then work together to act as particles of matter in different states, choosing suitable actions to show how the particles behave.

Teaching idea: Forces – force arrows

This starts as a simple game where children's movement is controlled by arrows drawn on the playground. As children walk around a path, an arrow pointing in the direction of travel might speed them up; an arrow pointing the opposite way might slow them down. Larger arrows can have a greater effect as they represent a larger force. Talk with children about how they might use force arrows to make them change direction.

Teaching idea: Electricity – how electricity flows

This is a playground version of the role play on page 115 of Chapter 9. Children can draw circuit diagrams for different circuits then act out how electricity will flow around them.

Figure 10.4 Using force arrows in playground science

Teaching idea: Earth and space – orbits

Children can draw the Sun, Earth and Moon, and arrows to show their interrelated orbits. They can then act out the yearly cycle with a fiery dance for the Sun, two or more children as the Earth rotating while orbiting the Sun, and then a smaller group or a single child as the Moon orbiting the Earth as it moves. A child acting as the Moon can keep their face towards the Earth as they orbit to show that the same side of the Moon always faces Earth.

Teaching idea: Sound – how sound travels

One child might be asked to bang a drum on the playground, and the others to listen and then describe what happens. They then can be asked to draw the drum and show with chalk how the sound travels. They may draw arrows, lines, curves and even concentric circles. The concentric circles are perhaps the best option as they look

Figure 10.5 Learners describe the orbit of the Moon around the Earth

similar to the concentric waves on a pool caused by a pebble thrown into the water. This is a good two-dimensional model of how sound travels in waves away from a sound source.

Useful discussion might consider the various options for representing the sound, how sound gets fainter as it travels and how that could be shown on the drawings.

Children's thoughts on playground science

Teacher: Does anything change about lessons when you go outside?

N: The way you do it changes . . . because inside everything has a limit to it. And when you're outside you don't have a limit because . . . well, you're outside. Well obviously you can't do whatever you want but . . . it makes it almost kind of limitless.

Conclusion

Playground science gives children a freedom to be creative. They can express science concepts in terms of actions or roles in a scenario or rules in a game. They are encouraged to make links between abstract concepts and concrete movements or diagrams. Risk taking is promoted as there is less sense of permanence, and ideas can be developed, corrected or even discarded as the form of the game or role play evolves.

The lesson then often spills over into playtime, with the children returning time and again to the drawings, alone and with others, rehearsing and teaching one another the science.

Chapter summary

- Playground science is a creative and effective teaching method.
- Children often continue to develop the activities at playtime.
- Playground science activities can be created for many different science topics.

11

Thinking frames

What will you learn from this chapter?
- Some examples of different thinking frames.
- How these examples work.
- How thinking frames can be used creatively.

A thinking frame is a structure for organizing thought. It can be used in the abstract, as a technique for thinking about a problem or a topic in a structured way, or in a more concrete form, as a written and therefore visual representation that helps to organize thinking. The structures described below can be used to develop and plan for writing, in which case they may be referred to as writing frames, a term that includes any format for structuring written work. Here we focus on the underlying thought processes and how these frames can be used creatively to reflect and structure understanding – hence the term 'thinking frames'.

These frames can be effective for an individual working alone to articulate and clarify their thinking around an area – for example, some people would use them when revising for an exam. Thinking frames often help us to retain knowledge because of the way they help us organize our ideas. For example, we see links differently when we see the whole picture. However, thinking frames are also very effective when used by groups who, through the frame, have a shared medium for expressing, reviewing and considering ideas.

Thinking frames are also inclusive as they can be used by those achieving highly to explore more complex ideas and links while, at the same time, helping others who are challenged by new ideas to consider, accommodate and assimilate them.

Figure 11.1 Thinking together

Thinking together

Sticky notes have already been mentioned in Chapter 3 as a method of organizing facts and questions with a class, but they are also a very useful tool for creative thinking in pairs and groups. With the contents of each note restricted to a single idea, fact, question or word, the mobility of the notes means that these concepts can be arranged then rearranged, categorized and then reorganized in many ways. This fluidity encourages children to visualize the underlying context from different perspectives. This encourages creativity as it makes it easier for children to make connections and comparisons, and allows them to use their intuition. Risk taking is also encouraged as anything that turns out to be unhelpful is easily undone. Flow charts, concept maps and many other graphic organizers can be created simply by joining sticky notes with lines or arrows drawn on more moveable notes. The result is a flexible, more creative structure than pen and paper normally allow.

Question matrix

Questioning is an important science skill that was also discussed in Chapter 3. It is a type of thinking some children find hard, and often their questions seek straightforward factual answers. How fast does sound travel? Which plant grows the fastest? Questioning skills can be developed by using a simple thinking frame that demonstrates how children can make their questions more creative. The question matrix in Figure 11.2 was designed by Chuck Wiederhold and illustrates a progression from

Higher-order thinking →

More open questions ↓

	WHAT event	WHERE or WHEN situation	WHICH choice	WHO person	WHY reason	HOW means
IS present	What is	When is	Which is	Who is	Why is	How is
DID past	What did	Where did	Which did	Who did	Why did	How did
CAN possibility	What can	When can	Which can	Who can	Why can	How can
WOULD probability	What would	Where would	Which would	Who would	Why would	How would
WILL prediction	What will	When will	Which will	Who will	Why will	How will
MIGHT Imagination	What might	Where might	Which might	Who might	Why might	How might

Figure 11.2 Example of a question matrix

Source: Wiederhold and Kagan (2007)

simple closed questions to those that are more complex and open (Wiederhold and Kagan, 2007). This matrix owes something to Bloom's (1956) original taxonomy of educational objectives. Children can attach their sticky note question to the section of the matrix that best describes it, and can be encouraged to add further higher-order questions. Similar question matrices are available online.

Here are some examples of questions of increasing complexity. We will use ice as the focus. Imagine that a group of children are observing a small and a large block of ice melting. There are some blanks here as not all the questions are relevant to every situation.

Higher-order thinking →

	WHAT event	WHERE or WHEN situation	WHICH choice	WHO person	WHY reason	HOW means
IS *present*	What is happening to the ice?		Which is colder?		Why is it melting?	How is it melting?
DID *past*	What was it like before it was frozen?	Where did the ice come from?	Which took longer to freeze?		Why did it become solid?	How did the water become solid?
CAN *possibility*	What can you do with ice?	Where can we find ice?	Which can I put in a cold drink?	Who can use ice?	Why can it change back?	How can ice stay frozen?
WOULD *probability*	What would happen if we put it on the radiator?	Would we find ice in hot paces?	Which would cool me down the most?	Who would need ice?	Why would the larger one melt slower?	How would we keep it frozen longer?
WILL *prediction*	What will happen to the ice?	When will it all be melted?	Which will melt first, the small block or the larger one?		Why will the smaller one melt faster?	How much water will it make?
MIGHT *imagination*	What might happen as it melts?	Where might it be used?	Which might melt first?	Who might like to have some ice?	Why might larger blocks of ice be more useful?	How might adding different solids affect melting ice?

More open questions ↓

Figure 11.3 Example of a question matrix for ice

Source: based on Wiederhold and Kagan (2007)

Teaching idea: Graphic organizers

For defining or describing a topic

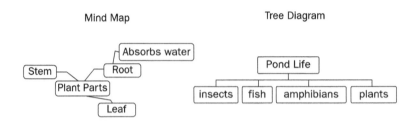

For making comparisons

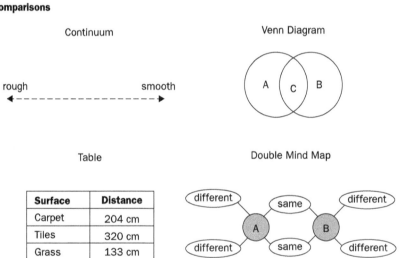

For showing a sequence

Figure 11.4 Graphic organizers

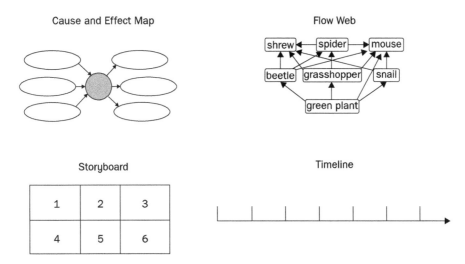

Figure 11.4 *continued*

Representing ideas and knowledge visually using diagrams, labels and arrows provides accessible, alternative and therefore potentially creative options for communication. Many first drafts of new ideas or structures are created this way as scribbles on the back of envelopes. Graphic organizers provide a way of refining this creativity. A variety of different organizers have been developed, each using techniques that are relevant to different types of problem. The tree diagram, flow chart and simple table are all well-known examples of graphic organizers, but there are many other types that can be useful in science teaching.

Some useful graphic organizers for science are shown in Figure 11.4.

Teaching idea: Being creative with graphic organizers

Ask children to work in groups to create a graphic organizer for a given topic; depending on their level of familiarity, the type of organizer used could be chosen by the group. Provide plenty of opportunity for the children to compare and analyse the work of other groups before using what they have learned to improve their own. As children get more used to how different organizers work, they can blend different elements of them together to suit the situation being represented. The most stimulating organizers use images and colour, often to summarize, categorize or link sections of the organizer, and children can even create symbolic icons to represent parts of their learning. Groups of children can use chalk to create graphic organizers they can then move around on in the playground (see the section on playground science in Chapter 10, page 127). Life-size thinking frames can be presented to the class by groups holding words and arrows on cards to demonstrate relationships or cause and effect.

Robert Marzano's (1998) important meta-study of research rated 4,000 different classroom strategies. The study found that, when students create graphical representations of what they are learning, it has an enormous positive effect on their progress. In fact, it was one of the most effective techniques in the study.

Teaching idea: Mind map

The mind map is a well-known tool for breaking down a topic into parts and showing how the parts are interrelated. Children can have the freedom to create many different mind maps for a given topic as the topic can be broken down in different ways. For example, a mind map on plants could have its main branches as the different parts and their functions, or as the different processes such as growth, pollination and seed dispersal. Mind maps are often referred to as concept maps, topic webs or spider diagrams, and usually include colour and images. They represent a very creative and flexible technique because, as children construct them, they are working in a similar way to how the brain works, making connections between areas of understanding with similar characteristics.

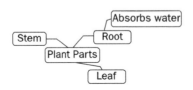

Figure 11.5 Mind map

Teaching idea: Tree diagram

A derivative of the mind map, the tree diagram has a similar structure but is useful for representing a hierarchy such as a family tree or the classification of living things. Tree diagrams can also be used to create a branching database or sorting key.

In one school, a class studying the topic of 'ourselves' chalked a branching database on the playground. The first question was written beside the playground entrance. Arrows led children to answers and further questions. The database showed them whether freckles are more likely with certain hair colours.

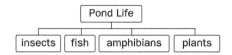

Figure 11.6 Tree diagram

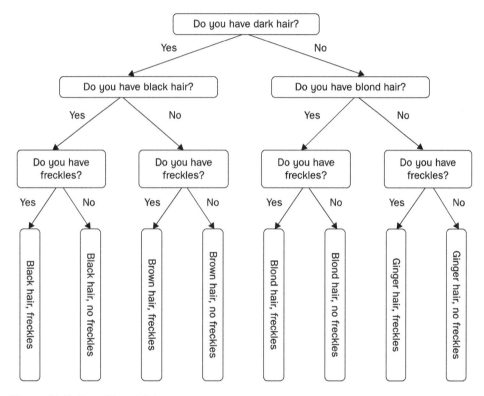

Figure 11.7 Branching database

Teaching idea: Continuum

A continuum is used to represent how something corresponds to a single criterion. For example, rocks can be placed in a line to show a comparison of texture, colour or simply size (see the section on sorting in Chapter 3, page 28). They can also display results from investigations: instruments can be displayed from quiet to loud, plants by how fast they grow, paper towels by how absorbent they are or how much they cost.

Figure 11.8 Continuum

The continuum can be used creatively as a non-numerical introduction to data handling for younger children. With older children, two continua crossed at right angles can be used to compare criteria and may reveal a corresponding relationship or a pattern – for example, 'Are more expensive paper towels more absorbent?' Scatter graphs and line graphs are simply crossed continua with numerical scales.

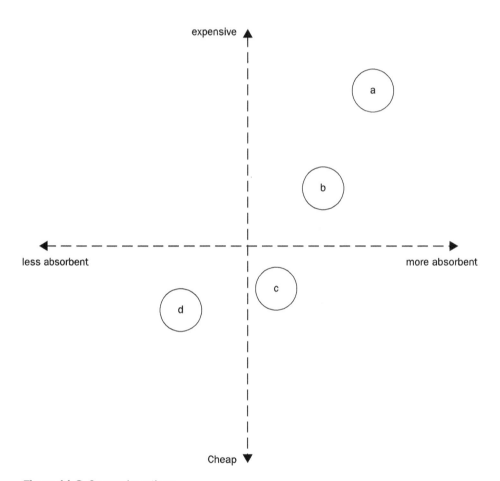

Figure 11.9 Crossed continua

Teaching idea: Venn diagrams

Useful for comparing sets of objects with similar criteria, the Venn diagram can be used when some of the objects in the groups share the characteristics of both sets: A = these objects are plastic; B = these objects are flexible; C = these objects are both plastic and flexible. (See Chapter 3, page 29, for how to get children to invent and create their own Venn diagrams.)

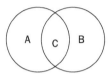

Figure 11.10 Venn diagram

Teaching idea: Tables

A table can be used to show a list of items and their characteristics – for example, how far a toy car travels on different surfaces after rolling down a ramp, or pairs of corresponding measurements such as the height of a plant and the number of days since planting.

Surface	Distance
Carpet	204 cm
Tiles	320 cm
Grass	133 cm

Figure 11.11 Table

Tables like this are very common in primary maths and science classes. The creativity will come in terms of when, where and how they are used. Strong links between maths and science might themselves be seen as creative, as would shifting responsibility for the construction of tables to the children. Tables can be presented as part of reports, articles, blogs, newsletters and displays. Groups could work on larger tables that even include samples of the material tested, e.g. carpet, tile, grass.

Teaching idea: Double mind map

Children often find it easier to identify differences than similarities. The structure of this mind map encourages children to recognize both. This thinking frame can be used to compare physical things, such as creatures or planets, but it can also be used more creatively to compare concepts. This is particularly useful when creating or analysing models and analogies (see Chapter 6, page 69).

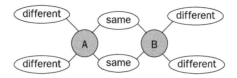

Figure 11.12 Double mind map

Teaching idea: Flow charts

In many thinking frames, simple lines can be used to create links between different parts of a concept. The introduction of arrows adds an extra element that can indicate causes, effects or some kind of flow – the flow of energy or, as seen in a life cycle, simply the flow of time. Showing children how arrows can represent these different variables gives them further creative tools to develop their own representations. They could combine a cause and effect map with a cycle to show the factors that affect the life cycle of a flowering plant. How about adding cause bubbles to a double mind map that compares the adaptation of two different animals? A cause bubble could show the environmental factors that have led to an adaptation being successful.

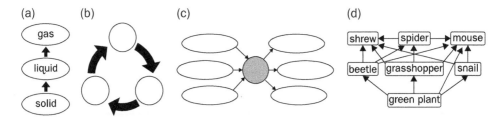

Figure 11.13 (a) Flow chart, (b) cycle, (c) cause and effect map, (d) flow web

Teaching idea: Storyboards

A storyboard is similar to a timeline in that both can be used to show changes or a sequence of events over time. They can be used to represent the stages of an investigation, which could be as creative as a comic-strip storyboard or as simple as a sequence of labelled diagrams on a timeline. Storyboards can also show a child's understanding of cause and effect within a scientific process. It can be helpful to create double storyboards or timelines to show the effects of taking different actions (see the Toothy Tina and Decay Dave example in Figure 11.15).

Figure 11.14 (a) Storyboard, (b) timeline

Figure 11.15 Use of a storyboard for science

Teaching idea: Using a SOLO taxonomy

The SOLO (structure of observed learning outcomes) taxonomy was developed by John Biggs and Kevin Collis in 1982. They were looking for a way to measure the understanding shown by a piece of work rather than the knowledge presented. They realized that the way work is structured demonstrates the level of understanding, and the resulting taxonomy breaks the development of understanding into five stages. These five stages are shown in Figure 11.16, which illustrates an example.

Pre-structural	The work shows no understanding of the topic. *I am not sure what a bulldozer is.*
Uni-structural 	The work shows understanding of one aspect of the topic. *Bulldozers can push things.*
Multi-structural 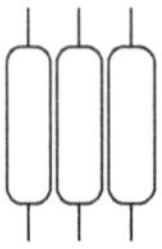	The work shows understanding of several aspects of the topic. *Other things can push or pull too. Bulldozers are big and strong. They can push really hard. People drive them.*
Relational 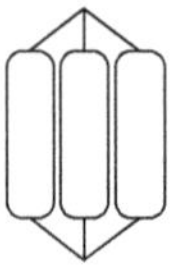	The work evaluates and makes links between several aspects of the topic. *The driver can control what to push in the bulldozer and how hard. I can push, like a bulldozer, to close a drawer or open a door and I can control how hard.*
Extended Abstract 	The work links several aspects of the topic and generalizes by making links with other topics. *A bulldozer's tracks push backwards and this pushes the bulldozer forwards. When I push a door there is a force on me pushing back. My push must be bigger to make the door move.*

Figure 11.16 The SOLO taxonomy

Source: adapted from Biggs and Collis (1982)

As the icons in Figure 11.16 show, the different stages represent how the brain works with a concept. The taxonomy develops from simple unrelated factual thinking about a topic to the relational stage where different ideas begin to be linked. Eventually we might progress to the extended abstract where a set of related ideas are considered in relation to other topics or higher principles. This last stage can take a long time to achieve and is generally considered to be the way in which experts think (Bransford, 2000).

Using SOLO creatively

In this model, one of the three key elements of creativity was the value of the work. The SOLO taxonomy offers us a scale that can be used to judge this.

Value

- I can use things I have already learned to help me.
- I stop and think about how I am doing in my work.
- I can spot problems and ways of dealing with them.
- I can see if my work has achieved its purpose.
- I can see how other people work to achieve their purposes.

Source: Redmond (2005)

Older children can be taught to peer assess and self-assess using the structure of SOLO, and the icons offer useful reminders at each stage.

Learning ladder

Younger children need a simpler strategy, and here SOLO can be adapted by the teacher to create 'learning ladders' that children can use to make value judgements about specific pieces of work. The effect of a learning ladder is similar to that of sharing a learning objective with children but, rather than being a single criterion to be met, it makes them aware of the progression of achievement possible within the task.

Figure 11.17 shows an example of a learning ladder used with Years 5 and 6 children for a piece of explanatory writing that described how different home-made instruments worked. From the bottom up, the first three statements are uni- and multi-structural, the fourth requires a relational response, and the top level is guiding children towards the extended abstract by asking them to link their work on instruments to their understanding of the principles of sound vibrations. Learning ladders work best when they are discussed beforehand and then displayed clearly as the children are working so they can review their progress.

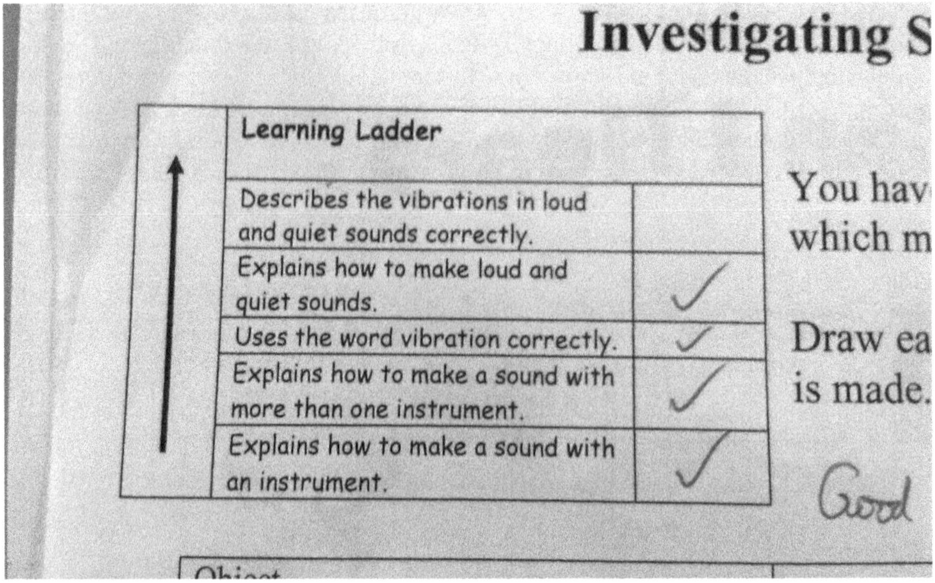

Figure 11.17 Learning ladder

Conclusion

Thinking frames present a powerful tool in a creative classroom. While the structures themselves are inherently creative, the way that they are used, and particularly the discussion that surrounds them, will maximize their creative learning potential. Give children the control to be imaginative and original in producing graphic organizers. Allow them the flexibility of sticky notes to take risks in their thinking. Both of these will encourage effective science learning. When coupled with the SOLO taxonomy or learning ladders, the children can also assess and see the value in their own learning and that of others.

Chapter summary

- There is great potential for learning and interactive collaboration using thinking frames such as graphic organizers or sticky notes that encourage flexibility and risk taking.

- Children can evaluate and refine their questions using a question matrix.

- Learning ladders and the SOLO taxonomy can help children develop metacognitive processes.

12

Cross-curricular science

What will you learn from this chapter?

- The current political background to cross-curricular learning.
- Why making cross-curricular links makes sense.
- Some examples of how to make effective and creative cross-curricular links with science.

The phrase 'cross-curricular learning' means different things to different people. It can mean a simple lesson with clear links to more than one subject – for example, a science lesson about heart rate that develops children's mathematical understanding of line graphs. Cross-curricular learning can also mean flexible, child-led project work and it can, of course, refer to a range of things between. To a few, however, it is simply seen as an opportunity to 'do pirates'!

Cross-curricular learning is described by Barnes (2011) as 'When the skills, knowledge and attitudes of a number of different disciplines are applied to a single experience, problem, question, theme or idea.' In this chapter we will look at a selection of cross-curricular links that, when planned well, can lead to effective and creative learning.

Background

The current political situation regarding cross-curricular work is an interesting one. In January 2008, Ed Balls, then Labour Secretary of State for Children, Schools and Families, asked Sir Jim Rose to lead an independent review of the primary curriculum. The final report was published in 2009, but the 2010 general election prevented the recommendations becoming law. The report strongly advocated cross-curricular learning:

> There are times when it is right to marshal content from different subjects into well-planned, cross-curricular studies. This is not only because it helps children to better understand ideas about such important matters as citizenship, sustainable development, financial capability and health and wellbeing, but also because it provides opportunities across the curriculum for them to use and apply what they have learned from the discrete teaching of subjects.
>
> (Rose, 2009: Executive Summary and Recommendations)

The recommendations of the Rose Review were widely welcomed by the educational establishment and many schools were quick to become more cross-curricular in their approach. The new Conservative-led coalition government, however, was not happy with the report and launched its own review of the National Curriculum in 2011. This resulted in a new National Curriculum (DfE, 2013), statutory from September 2014, which has a clear emphasis on discrete subject learning.

However, the new National Curriculum does not dismiss cross-curricular teaching altogether. Within the science section, for example, there is encouragement for teachers who want to show children the relevance of their learning:

> ... teachers will wish to use different contexts to maximize their pupils' engagement with and motivation to study science.

As schools are required to teach only the specified content for science by the end of a key stage, there is leeway in the structure of the curriculum that allows teachers to plan creatively to maximize links with other subjects:

> Within each key stage, schools therefore have the flexibility to introduce content earlier or later than set out in the programme of study. In addition, schools can introduce key stage content during an earlier key stage if appropriate.

In fact, cross-curricular links with English and maths are emphasized in the National Curriculum; it specifies that teachers are to develop pupils' numeracy, oracy and literacy skills across all subjects.

Why teach cross-curricular science?

The distinctions between subjects are artificial and, to some extent, arbitrary. Is rainfall geography or science? Is a shoe shop sales report numeracy or literacy? In reality both are both; the world outside the classroom is a cross-curricular place. So, is discrete subject teaching the best preparation for the world? Many would argue that it is not, that discrete subject teaching tends to make learning appear irrelevant to many, isolated from their everyday lives.

Cross-curricular learning supports the constructivist theory of education (e.g. Vygotsky, 1978). If we build our understanding of the world through experience then how better to deepen our comprehension than through experiences from a range of perspectives? A more holistic view of the world is available through cross-curricular learning than from a narrow-sighted, subject-specific viewpoint.

We saw in Chapter 6 how the brain learns by making physical links between neurons. In this way neural networks are created that embody our understanding of a concept (Petty, 2009). The more links this network has, the greater the number of associations with interrelated concepts, the deeper our understanding of the idea. It is logical then to suppose that cross-curricular learning develops and encourages this link-making activity within the brain and leads to deeper understanding. While Barnes (2011) points out that scientific research is only just beginning to reveal how the brain works and we should be cautious about any deductions we make, he is happy to conclude that neuroscience supports the principles of cross-curricular learning.

Cross-curricular learning and creativity

Cross-curricular learning supports creativity because it fosters imaginative thought. As children get used to seeing things from different perspectives they are encouraged to explore alternatives and make comparisons in their own thinking. This 'integration' of different perspectives, or different ways of thinking about concepts, was included by Sternberg (2003) as one of nine distinct types of creativity. Cross-curricular learning also encourages originality as children become aware that there are often multiple routes to achieving an outcome, and become confident to experiment with new and unusual responses and ideas.

> **Teaching Tip**
>
> **Planning for creativity**
> *Plan choices* – build in opportunities for children to make decisions.
> *Consider alternatives* – plan for a range of outcomes.
> *Be flexible* – don't always stick to the plan.

Making cross-curricular science effective

Successful cross-curricular science requires relevant, creative and accurate links between subjects. These links tend to work both ways; they are concepts that precipitate learning in both subjects. There is a temptation in this kind of work to make links wherever possible. However, tenuous links should be avoided. They do little to reinforce either learning or creativity, and can lead to misconceptions. Consider the examples below. Which is the more effective link?

Link A: Viking longships and materials

Which material would be best to make a boat?

Comparing possible boat-making materials such as wood, cardboard, metal foil and plasticine provides a great opportunity for learning about the properties of different materials, yet linking this investigation to Viking longships is tenuous and unhelpful. From the investigation, children are likely to conclude that the best material is either metal foil or plasticine – two materials that are easy for children to make into boat shapes and that are fairly water resistant. A boat made from either would work well in a bowl in the classroom. However, the Vikings obviously used wood. They had no access to the other materials and, although wood is difficult to shape in comparison to the other materials, they needed seaworthy craft that were both large and strong. Making a full-sized longship from metal foil or plasticine is plainly ridiculous. So, in reality, the science investigation here has very little to teach us about Vikings.

Link B: Viking longships and water resistance

Which shape makes the best boat?

Using plasticine to investigate the best shape for a boat can explain why the Vikings used longships. Children can compare shorter, wider boats with more streamlined, longer boats and observe the effect of water resistance on both. This investigation would help them to come to a useful conclusion about the reason for the shape of a Viking longship. This, then, is a strong link. It teaches about both science and about the Vikings. The science is learned in context, and the history is discovered by the children in a practical and creative way.

The activity in the second scenario is very similar to that in the first, yet the change in emphasis makes a great difference to the children's learning. Careful planning is therefore crucial to ensure that the cross-curricular links made are productive for learning.

Planning for cross-curricular science

The example cross-curricular links above highlight the precision required in cross-curricular work; it requires time for careful and considered planning. This planning can be a creative and enjoyable process for teachers but, as we are all too aware, there are a great many demands on a teacher's time and it is not unknown for planning, on occasion, to be rushed. In this situation we would argue that discrete subject teaching has an advantage. Without the requirement to think across subjects, planning for discrete subject teaching is more straightforward.

A major complexity with cross-curricular planning is in ensuring curriculum coverage. If taught topics need to link strongly with others to create a working theme, then what about those areas of the curriculum that are difficult to fit in? We could be left at the end of the year with a collection of disconnected bits and pieces to get through. The other side of this coin is the many topics that link well to many others and therefore risk duplication. There is a risk that children could find themselves repeating the topic of materials term by term, year by year, through themes such as clothing, buildings, toys in the past, etc.

Carefully thought through long-term planning can get around these issues, and starting by choosing themes from a range of different subjects helps. Science itself contains many great cross-curricular themes that link strongly with history, geography, music, design and technology, physical education, and computing. We will explore these ideas in detail below.

It would seem therefore that the most sensible approach to take to cross-curricular work would be a compromise. Creative cross-curricular planning can be used where there is time to create meaningful, well thought out links within the context of a detailed long-term plan, but discrete subject lessons may also be required where specific skills such as writing and maths can be practised before being put to use within the cross-curricular themes.

Science and the core skills

Before we look at links with foundation subjects it will be helpful to say a little about how science can support the learning of core numeracy and literacy skills, as well as the skills required in using information and communication technology (ICT).

Science provides the perfect context in which to integrate the skills learned separately in maths and English lessons. These three subjects complement one another perfectly as scientists need to use a range of mathematical and language skills to investigate, communicate their findings and document the scientific process.

An enquiry involving temperature, for example, is a perfect opportunity to re-inforce children's skills in reading scales and their understanding of negative numbers. Carefully planned teacher questions will make the links explicit and ensure they carry two-way traffic. How much colder is it in the freezer than in the classroom? Can you use what we have learned about negative numbers to calculate the difference? Data handling is an obvious area where mathematical skills can be learned in the context of a science lesson, from simply recording in a table to tally charts, pictograms and scatter graphs.

English skills, too, can be embedded within science lessons. Science topics such as sound provide opportunities for writing short explanations. Children could explain how and why instruments can play different notes or, more specifically, about the vibrations of sounds of different pitches and volumes. Science can provide a back-ground for non-chronological reports, biographies and even descriptive writing, which can, in turn, encourage more detailed observation. Most usefully, and perhaps most seamlessly, science provides numerous opportunities for speaking and listening. The sharing and discussion of ideas within small groups and with the whole class has been a constant theme throughout many chapters of this book, and expressing ideas verbally is a key aspect of effective learning in science.

While the subject title 'computing' has taken over in National Curriculum 2014 (DfE, 2013), children are still expected to be able to use and express themselves through information and communication technology. Here science can provide opportunities to use spreadsheets and graphing programs to handle data, to organize and classify information using databases, to record and edit images and sound digitally, to create models or simulations using graphical modelling, animation or programming software, and to present the findings of scientific enquiry through presentations or word processing. See Chapter 4 (page 39) for more on using computers in science.

Science is an inherently cross-curricular subject. Many of these core skills are fully integrated into science learning and the scientific process would not be possible without them. Despite this, there is still a need for careful planning. These implicit links are made far more effective when the teacher is fully aware of them. The specific learning from other subjects that can be applied should be highlighted and discussed with the children within the lesson.

Examples of cross-curricular science

Science and history

In the non-statutory guidance of the National Curriculum (DfE, 2013) there are many references to historical scientists and inventors; people such as Alhazen and Copernicus, who studied the solar system, famous names like Darwin and Newton sit alongside less well-known figures such as the animal behaviourist Jane Goodall, the palaeontologist Mary Anning and the inventor of wrinkle-free cotton, Ruth Benerito. These are just a few of the recommended names – in theory, the whole science curriculum could be covered through a historical study of the scientists and inventors who theorized, tested, invented and developed ideas, creating the body of knowledge that is science today. This is not recommended. However, children's understanding of both science and history topics can be greatly enhanced by placing the science in its historical context.

Alhazen, for example, was a renowned Arab scientist who was born in Basra, Iraq, and lived during the Islamic Golden Age. He is credited as a major influence in the science of optics and on the use of practical experiments in science.

The lives of Mary Seacole and Florence Nightingale in Victorian times provide a compelling context to understanding both the Victorians' values and their understanding of the effects of hygiene on health.

More famous names will be mentioned below, but we will not attempt to create an exhaustive list of interesting lives here. There is a selection of useful people listed in Chapter 5 (page 65).

Teaching idea: Plants – part of a plant or flower

Art, Design and Technology

A study of plants or flowers could be usefully linked to artists who painted detailed pictures of flowers, such as Van Gogh, Monet and Georgia O'Keeffe. A similar link could be made with the Victorian William Morris, whose textile designs show clear details of stems, leaves and flowers.

Teaching idea: Living things and their habitats – habitats and adaptations

Art

Camouflage is a topic that encompasses both science and art. Children can learn from nature about the techniques and uses of camouflage, and use their learning to create artwork that reflects this understanding.

Teaching idea: Animals, including humans – bones and muscles

The Olympics of Ancient Greece provides an excellent context for links between science, art, history and PE. Children can talk about how our skeleton and muscles support us and allow us to move in different ways to compete in different Olympic events. Ancient Greek art was dominated by representations of the human body in sculpture and on pottery.

Art, History, PE

Teaching idea: Animals, including humans – the circulatory system and exercise

The theme of sport allows for strong links between science and PE, especially the link between health and exercise. It is also useful for investigating the circulatory system and pulse rate. During exercise, the heart beats faster and we breathe more rapidly because our muscles require more oxygen, which is delivered by the blood. Investigations into the effects of different types of exercise on pulse rate are enhanced by an understanding of the reasons why the body reacts as it does.

PE

Teaching idea: Animals, including humans – healthy eating

The topic of healthy eating links directly to working with food in design and technology. Children can design and make healthy drinks, sandwiches or salads based on their understanding of food groups.

Design and Technology

Teaching idea: Animals, including humans – ourselves

As mentioned above, the work of Florence Nightingale and Mary Seacole sheds light on life in Victorian times, and creates opportunities for links to science learning about health, hygiene and parts of the body.

History

Teaching idea: Materials – properties of materials

Art

Many material properties can be explored using art techniques. Observational drawing encourages children to look closely at both texture and colour, while texture and shape can be explored using objects as shapes for printing or by taking rubbings. Children can make creative choices about different materials and how they might be used in art. Which materials can be used for applying paint or as an alternative to paper? Which materials are flexible enough to use as an alternative to clay for modelling? How might other materials be shaped or joined for sculpture?

Teaching idea: Materials – uses of materials

History

There is a strong link between the uses of different materials and historical enquiry into the Stone Age, Bronze Age or Iron Age. Stones such as flint and slate were both used to make tools in the Stone Age, but bone was also used. Granite was useful for buildings and monuments. The discovery of bronze led to a new era, defined by stronger, better tools and weapons, a cycle that repeated again as smiths learned to strengthen iron with carbon to make steel, a significant improvement over bronze. Throughout these periods other interesting materials were used, such as animal skin and leather for clothing, as well as wood, wicker, wattle and daub, and thatch for building dwellings.

Teaching idea: Rocks – fossils

Art

In addition to the science link between fossils and evolution and inheritance, there is a strong link that can be made with natural art. The children can look at the work of the artist Andy Goldsworthy, and his use of pattern, line and texture, to create their own artwork based on fossil patterns.

Teaching idea: Seasonal change – weather

Geography

An inherent link in the National Curriculum (DfE, 2013) is that within the topic of seasonal change. An understanding of the seasons is as much geography as science.

Within the curriculum, however, the topic is restricted to Key Stage 1; extending it into Key Stage 2 could create meaningful links to seasonal changes in different climates and weather patterns around the world, as well as climate change.

Teaching idea: Light – light sources, light and dark

Van Gogh's painting *Starry Night* makes an excellent discussion point when learning about light sources. Other useful links here are the way different artists use light and shade in paintings, and the work of light artists such as James Turrell.

Art

Find out more about James Turrell at this website:

www.jamesturrell.com/ (tinyurl.com/lxcr8y7)

Teaching idea: Sound – making instruments

Percussion instruments such as a shaker or drum can be constructed from a small container holding rice or dried peas, or from a balloon pulled tight over a plastic pot. These can be used to learn about vibrations being the source of sound, and that larger vibrations make louder sounds. Making tuned instruments to learn about pitch is trickier, however. Strong glass bottles or beakers filled with different levels of water and tapped gently can, with patience, be tuned to different notes, as can cardboard tubes cut to different lengths and tapped on a table. A set of rulers held down by heavy books and protruding over the edge of the table by different amounts will also produce notes of different pitches and, in this case, close observation can reveal the slower speed of the vibration of the lower notes.

Design and Technology

Teaching idea: Electricity – circuits and switches

Circuits can be used to create or enhance children's models made in design and technology. Lego® houses can be illuminated and alarmed. Cardboard torches can be built. Cars or buggies or K'Nex® structures can be motorized. A simple bent-wire buzzer game is quick to build and use, and could be extended by children to create a simplified version of the classic game Operation. 'Can you pick up all the peas with the

Design and Technology

chopsticks without setting off the buzzer?' This is an example that uses chopsticks and a plate covered with metal foil and wired into a buzzer circuit.

Making simple switches is an effective way to learn about conductors and insulators, and children will be keen to create their own designs.

Teaching idea: Earth in space – day and night

Geography

There is a clear link between the science topic of night and day and the geographical concept of time zones and lines of longitude. Observing live webcams of places in different time zones and acting out the actions of people in different parts of the world are two relevant activities discussed in detail in Chapter 4 and Chapter 6, respectively.

Teaching idea: Earth in space – the orbits of the Earth and Moon

History

As mentioned above, Alhazen was an important scientist of the Islamic Golden Age. He was among the first to realize the importance of practical work in that it provided essential evidence for theories. However, he was also an early pioneer in astronomy and was critical of errors in Ptolemy's descriptions of the geocentric model of the solar system. He was one of the first scientists to propose that the Earth rotates on its axis.

Conclusion

Creativity is often plain to see in young children who are learning about the world through play and exploration. Similar skills are required for practical scientific enquiry, and cross-curricular topics can provide this learning with a meaningful context.

Chapter summary

- Cross-curricular learning can create deeper understanding of a topic.
- Planning cross-curricular topics carefully can support creative learning.
- Combining cross-curricular work and discrete subject lessons can be an effective compromise.

Bibliography

Allen, M. (2010) *Misconceptions in Primary Science*. London: Open University Press/McGraw-Hill Education.

Asoko, H. and de Bóo, M. (2001) *Representing Ideas in Science Through Analogies and Illustrations* (rev. edn 2008). Hatfield: Association for Science Education.

Baines, E., Davies, C. and Blatchford, P. (2009) Improving pupil group work interaction and dialogue in primary classrooms: results from a year-long intervention study. *Cambridge Journal of Education*, 39(1): 95–117.

Barnes, J. (2011) *Cross-curricular Learning 3–11*. London: Sage.

Baud, D. (ed.) (1987) *Developing Student Autonomy in Learning*. London: Routledge.

Bianchi, L. and Feasey, R. (2011) *Science Beyond the Classroom Boundaries for 4–7 Year Olds*. Maidenhead: Open University Press.

Biggs, J. and Collis, K. (1982) *Evaluating the Quality of Learning*. New York: Academic Press.

Bloom, B.S. (1956) *Taxonomy of Educational Objectives, Handbook 1: The Cognitive Domain*. New York: David McKay Co., Inc.

Boyd, M. (2013) Journey to the outdoors. *Primary Science*, 129, September/October. Hatfield: Association for Science Education.

Bransford, J.D. (2000) *How People Learn: Brain, Mind, Experience and School*. Washington, DC: National Research Council.

Bucknall, S. (2012) *Children as Researchers in Primary Schools*. London/New York: Routledge.

Burrs, S. (2012) Models and analogues: how useful are they? *Primary Science*, 123, May/June. Hatfield: Association for Science Education: 15–18.

Collins, R. (2013) Interconnecting with VIPs. *Primary Science*, 130, November/December. Hatfield: Association for Science Education: 12–15.

Computing at School (2013) *Computing in the National Curriculum: A Guide for Primary Teachers*. London: NACCCE.

Creative Partnerships (2005) *Building Creative Futures: The Story of the Creative Action Research Awards*. London: Arts Council England.

Cross, A. (2000) Pedagogy and curricular subjects: the case of design and technology as part of primary education. Unpublished dissertation, University of Manchester.

Cross, A. (2012) ITT teach! *Primary Science*. Morecambe: CC-Apps. Available online at: http://www.cc-apps.co.uk/page/109/Science.htm.

Cross, A. and Bowden, A. (2009) *Essential Primary Science*. Maidenhead: Open University Press.

Csikszentmihalyi, M. (1996) *Creativity: Flow and the Psychology of Discovery and Invention*. New York: Harper.

Dann, R. (2013) Be curious: understanding 'curiosity' in contemporary curriculum policy and practice. *Education 3–13*, 41(6): 557–561.

Davies, D. (2011) *Teaching Science Creatively*. London: Routledge.

Department for Education (DfE) (2013) *The National Curriculum*. London: DfE.

Feasey, R. (2007) *Primary Science for Teaching Assistants*. Abingdon: David Fulton.

Flavell, J. (1979) Metacognition and cognitive monitoring: a new area of cognitive-development inquiry. *American Psychologist*, 34(10): 906–911.

Galton, M. and Hargreaves, L. (2009) Group work: still a neglected art? *Cambridge Journal of Education*, 39(1): 1–6.

Goldsworthy, A. and Feasey, R. (1994) *Making Sense of Primary Science Investigations*. Hatfield: Association for Science Education.

Grainger, T. and Barnes, J. (2006). Creativity in the primary curriculum, in Arthur, J., Grainger, T. and Wray, D. (eds) *Learning to Teach in the Primary School*. London: Routledge: 209–225.

Harlen, W. (1999) *Effective Teaching of Science*. Edinburgh: Scottish Council for Research in Education.

Harlen, W. (2006) Assessment for learning and assessment of learning, in Harlen, W. (ed.) *ASE Guide to Primary Science Education*. Hatfield: Association for Science Education.

Harlen, W., Macro, C., Kathleen, R. and Schilling, M. (2003) *Making Progress in Primary Science*. London: RoutledgeFalmer.

Harrison, C. and Harlen, W. (2006) Children's self- and peer assessment, in Harlen, W. (ed.) *ASE Guide to Primary Science Education*. Hatfield: Association for Science Education.

Hattie, J. (2009) *Visible Learning*. London: Routledge.

Hattie, J., Biggs, J. and Purdie, N. (1996) Effects of learning skills interventions on student learning: a meta-analysis. *Review of Educational Research*, 66(2): 99–136.

Howe, C. and Mercer, N. (2007) *Children's Social Development, Peer Interaction and Classroom Learning*. Cambridge: University of Cambridge. Available online at: www.primaryreview. org.uk (accessed 23 September 2013).

Johnson, J. (2008) Can children be creative in science? *Teaching Thinking and Creativity*, 8.1(22). Available online at: http://www.bishopg.ac.uk/docs/Profiles/Johnston_TTC22_pg42_47_Can_children_be_creative.pdf.

Jones, R. and Wyse, D. (2013) *Creativity in the Primary Curriculum*. London: Routledge.

Kagan, S. (1990) The structural approach to cooperative learning. *Educational Leadership*, 47(4): 12–15.

Kellett, M. (2005) *How to Develop Children as Researchers*. London: Sage.

Kutnick, P., Hodgkinson, S., Sebba, J., Humphreys, S., Galton, M., Steward, S., Blatchford, P. and Baines, E. (2007) Pupil grouping strategies and practices at Key Stage 2 and 3. *Research Report 796*. Nottingham: DfES Publications.

Longshaw, S. (2009) Creativity in science teaching. *School Science Review*, 190. Hatfield: Association for Science Education: 91–94.

Lunn, S. (2006) Working like real scientists. *Primary Science*, 94, September/October. Hatfield: Association for Science Education: 4–7.

Maloney, J. and Curtis, S. (2012) Using models to promote children's scientific understanding. *Primary Science*, 123, May/June. Hatfield: Association for Science Education: 5–7.

Marzano, R.J. (1998) *A Theory Based Meta-analysis of Research on Instruction*. Aurora, Colorado: Mid-continent Research for Education and Learning.

Milne, A.A. (1926) *Winnie-the-Pooh*. London: Puffin.

NACCCE (1999) *All Our Futures: Creativity, Culture and Education*. London: NACCCE. Available online at: http://sirkenrobinson.com/pdf/allourfutures.pdf.

Naylor, S. and Keogh, B. (2010) *Concept Cartoons in Science Education*. Sandbach: Millgate House.

Novak, J.D. and Gowin, D.B. (1984) *Learning how to Learn*. New York: Cambridge University Press.

Ofsted (2013) *Maintaining Curiosity*. London: Ofsted. Available online at: http://www.ofsted. gov.uk/resources/maintaining-curiosity-survey-science-education-schools.

Osbourne, R.J. and Freyberg, P. (1985) *Learning in Science: The Implications of 'Children's Science'*. New Zealand: Heinemann.

Oversby, J. (2012) *ASE Guide to Research in Science Education*. Hatfield: Association for Science Education.

Petty, G. (2009) *Evidence-based Teaching: A Practical Approach*. Cheltenham: Nelson Thornes.

Pinker, S. (1999) *How the Mind Works*. London: Allen Lane/Penguin Press.

Raje, S. and Barleson, E. (2013) Getting third graders to put on their science 'thinking caps'. *Primary Science*, 130, November/December. Hatfield: Association for Science Education: 29–31.

Redmond, C. (2005) *The Creativity Wheel: The Framework for Assessing Pupil Development*. Durham: Creative Partnerships and the Arts Council.

Robinson, K. (2006) *How Schools Kill Creativity*. Film available online at: http://www.ted.com/ talks/ken_robinson_says_schools_kill_creativity.html.

Rose, Sir J. (2009) *Independent Review of the Primary Curriculum: Final Report*. Nottingham: DCFS Publications. Available online at: http://publications.teachernet.gov.uk/eordering-download/primary_curriculum_report.pdf (accessed 3 January 2014).

Ross, K. (2013) Let the children talk. *Primary Science*, 129, September/October. Hatfield: Association for Science Education: 31–33.

Sawyer, R.K. (2004). Creative teaching: collaborative discussion as disciplined improvisation. *Educational Researcher*, 33: 12–20.

Serret, N. (2006) Developing children's thinking in primary science, in Harlen, W. (ed.) *ASE Guide to Primary Science Education*. Hatfield: Association for Science Education.

Simon, S., Naylor, S., Keogh, B., Maloney, J. and Downing, B. (2008) Puppets promoting engagement and talk in science. *International Journal of Science Education*, 30(9): 1229–1248.

Spendlove, D. and Cross, A. (2012) Design and technology, in Jones, R. and Wyse, D. (eds) *Creativity in the Primary Curriculum*. London: David Fulton.

Sternberg, R. (2003) *Wisdom, Intelligence and Creativity Synthesised*. Cambridge: Cambridge University Press.

Tompson, C. (2008) Difficult to sit still. *Primary Science*, 103, May/June. Hatfield: Association for Science Education: 4–7.

Turner, J. (2012) It's not fair! *Primary Science*, 121, January/February. Hatfield: Association for Science Education: 30–33.

Vygotsky, L.S. (1978) *Mind in Society: The Development of Higher Mental Processes*. Cambridge, MA: Harvard University Press.

Vygotsky, L.S. (1986) An experimental study of the development of concepts, in Kozulin, A. (ed.) *Thought and Language*. Cambridge, MA: MIT Press.

Ward, H. (2011) Creativity for a purpose. *Primary Science*, 119, September/October. Hatfield: Association for Science Education: 5–7.

Wiederhold, C. and Kagan, S. (2007) *Cooperative Learning and Higher-level Thinking: The Q-Matrix* (rev. Australian edn). Heatherton, Victoria: Hawker Brownlow Education.

Wyse, D. and Dowson, P. (2009) *The Really Useful Creativity Book*. London: Routledge.

Index

Locators shown in *italics* refer to figures and tables.

ESSENTIAL PRIMARY SCIENCE 2/e

Alan Cross and Adrian Bowden

2014
9780335263349 - Paperback

eBook also available

If you are teaching - or learning - to teach primary science, this is the toolkit to support you!

Highly respected and widely used, Essential Primary Science 2E blends essential subject knowledge with a vast array of teacher activities. Updated and revised throughout to reflect the requirements of the new National Curriculum, it covers the essential knowledge and understanding that you need; plus it offers over 200 great ideas for teaching primary science at KSI and KS2 - so no more late nights thinking up creative new ways to teach key concepts!

Written in a friendly and supportive style this new edition offers:

- Over 200 original and new activities to complement the new curriculum, ready for you to try out in the classroom
- Tips on how to ensure each lesson includes both practical and investigative elements
- Suggestions on how to make your lessons engaging, memorable and inclusive
- How to deal with learners' common scientific misconceptions in each topic
- Two new chapters on working scientifically and how to tackle assessment
- New up-to-date web links to quality free resources

Drawing on their own extensive teaching experience and understanding of the new National Curriculum, the authors provide the essential guide to teaching primary science for both trainee teachers and qualified teachers who are not science specialists.

www.openup.co.uk

OPEN UNIVERSITY PRESS
McGraw - Hill Education

ENHANCING PRIMARY SCIENCE
Developing Effective Cross-Curricular Links

Lois Kelly and Di Stead

9780335247042 (Paperback)
2012

eBook also available

This book gives helpful insights into why making effective cross-curricular links enriches science and discusses when and how to make effective and authentic links between science and other subjects. Each chapter tackles a particular subject and considers how it can enhance science learning through a variety of approaches and a wealth of ideas for the classroom.

Key features:

- Includes contributions from a range of expert practitioners
- Provides a good balance between theory and practice
- Includes practical advice and tasks to help develop your confidence and skill in cross-curricular teaching

www.openup.co.uk

PRIMARY SCIENCE
Teaching the Tricky Bits

Neil Rutledge

9780335222285 (Paperback)
2010

eBook also available

The book provides a combination of engaging, practical lesson ideas and subject knowledge to help you teach the trickiest parts of primary science such as materials and their properties, magnetism, circuits, forces and life processes. The book includes a range of accessible ideas, hints and tips with a focus on providing a skills-based, problem-solving approach to learning.

Each topic area includes advice on:

- How to link the topic with other areas of learning
- Identifying and challenging common misconceptions
- How to effectively pre-assess the learners' ideas to best meet their needs
- Practical activities for challenging and developing children's ideas
- Explanatory models to help pupils consolidate their understanding

www.**openup**.co.uk

OPEN UNIVERSITY PRESS
McGraw - Hill Education